BORN IN 1963

WORD SEARCH

THIS BOOK

BELONGS TO

••

ELIZABETH ABSALOM & MALCOLM WATSON

D'AZUR PUBLISHING

BORN IN 1963 WORD SEARCH

Published by D'Azur Publishing 2022
D'Azur Publishing is a Division of D'Azur Limited

First published in Great Britain in 2022 by D'Azur Limited
Contact: info@d-azur.com Visit www.d-azur.com
ISBN 9798848989328

ACKNOWLEDGEMENTS

The publisher wishes to acknowledge the following people and sources:

British Newspaper Archive; The Times Archive; Front Cover Malcolm Watson; p4 Dean Hochman; p10 Digital Monkey; p10 Durham Weather Station; p18 Dave Wheeler; p18 Dr Julian Paren; p18 Shetland.org; p18 David Gifford; p34 Start Safety; p38 Rowland Scherman; p42 Medway Queen Preservation Society; p46 Classic Cars (Rover and Hillman); p46 Drive-my (Triumph); p50 CBT Stunt Alliance; p54 Imperial War Museum; p29 Fin Fahey; p54 Chase Evans; p56 Victor Hugo King; p56 NASA; p58 eBat; 94 Quatro Valvole;

Whilst we have made every effort to contact copyright holders, should we have made any omission, please contact us so that we can make the appropriate acknowledgement.

CONTENTS

Every puzzle is based on the stories printed on the facing page.

EASIER puzzles have words that go horizontally forwards and backwards and also upwards and downwards. Letters may be used in more than one word.

HARDER puzzles have words that can go in any direction - horizontally, vertically and diagonally, both forwards and backwards. Letters may be used in more than one word.

LIFE IN 1963 - PART 1

Monarch - Queen Elizabeth II

Prime Minister Harold Macmillan until October 19th then Alec Douglas-Home. Both Conservative.

In 1963 Harold Macmillan was presiding over a period where individual events made it a watershed in Britain's post war history. In June, in the aftermath of the biggest scandal in politics, the 'Profumo Affair', he was so bewildered by the madness of this new age that he could only brokenly stammer to the Commons, 'I do not live among young people fairly widely.'

Labour MPs were clamouring for him to resign, and his own party hastened his political doom. It was the end of the 'old order'; the winter of The Big Freeze; Saturday night satire with TW3; President de Gaulle slamming the door on joining the Common Market; Dr Beeching closing the railways; the Great Train Robbery; Polaris; Dr Who appearing and the assassination of John F Kennedy.

But perhaps, it was mostly the Year of the Beatles. The mop-topped four released their first album, 'Please Please Me' and Beatlemania takes hold across Britain.

FAMOUS PEOPLE WHO WERE BORN IN 1963

26th Jan: José Mourinho, football manager
17th Feb: Alison Hargreaves, British climber
27th Mar: Quentin Tarantino, film maker
8th April: Julian Lennon, Singer
11th May: Natasha Richardson, British actress
25th June: George Michael, British singer
3rd July: Tracey Emin, British artist
3rd Nov: Ian Wright, British footballer
5th Dec: Eddie 'The Eagle' Edwards, skier

FAMOUS PEOPLE WHO DIED IN 1963

18th Jan: Hugh Gaitskell, British politician
29th Jan: Robert Frost, American poet
11th Feb: Sylvia Plath, American poet
5th Mar: Patsy Cline, American singer
22nd Aug: William Morris, founder, Morris cars
10th Oct: Edith Piaf, French singer
22nd Nov: John F Kennedy, President, USA
22nd Nov: Aldous Huxley, Author
22nd Nov: CS Lewis, Irish born British writer

LIFE IN 1963 - EASIER

```
G  A  I  T  S  K  E  L  L  P  J  J  D  C  L
F  P  F  A  I  P  H  T  I  D  E  P  I  T  Y
C  N  H  U  N  E  L  L  U  A  G  E  D  H  C
P  L  H  S  N  R  H  E  X  O  U  T  P  E  K
Y  H  T  Q  E  Z  E  E  R  F  G  I  B  B  O
A  U  E  R  V  B  Q  E  Y  D  E  N  N  E  K
W  T  B  Y  W  V  H  M  D  P  V  H  Z  A  J
L  W  A  P  R  O  F  U  M  O  Y  R  L  T  E
I  Z  Z  F  S  R  T  Y  W  M  N  Z  E  L  R
A  L  I  R  E  L  G  A  E  E  H  T  N  E  K
R  D  L  O  R  A  H  O  O  S  U  B  N  S  K
M  N  E  D  G  D  R  W  H  O  V  C  O  O  F
J  F  G  F  E  N  I  L  C  T  H  N  N  H  X
V  V  C  S  L  E  W  I  S  C  E  B  S  D  U
V  T  P  N  A  L  L  I  M  C  A  M  Z  H  K
```

HAROLD	**MACMILLAN**	**ELIZABETH**	**PROFUMO**
BIG FREEZE	**DE GAULLE**	**RAILWAY**	**DR WHO**
KENNEDY	**THE BEATLES**	**THE EAGLE**	**LENNON**
EDITH PIAF	**CS LEWIS**	**GAITSKELL**	**CLINE**

LIFE IN 1963 - PART 2

Born in 1963, you were one of 53.6 million people living in Britain and your life expectancy *then* was 70 years. You were one of the 18.3 births per 1,000 population and you had a 2.2% chance of dying as an infant, a rapidly declining chance as this figure in 1950 was almost 31%.

You were at the beginning of an exciting era of individualism, young people had found their voice and were heard. It was the tentative beginning of the feminist movement, saw the growth in campaigns against nuclear weapons and the war in Vietnam and in America, the racial intolerance brought to the fore, the civil rights leader Martin Luther King.

Edward Craven-Walker invented his psychedelic Astro (lava) amp in 1963. The idea came from an egg-timer he saw in a Dorset pub that was made by a regular. Edward envisaged he could illuminate and heat a 'non-mixing' special coloured wax in a clear or translucent liquid to create a visual ornament.

How Much Did It Cost?

The Average Pay:	£860	(£17 p.w)
The Average House:	£3,160	
Loaf of White Bread:	1s 2½ d	(6p)
Pint of Milk:	8½ d	(3p)
Pint of Beer:	2s 1d	(10½p)
Dozen Eggs:	4s	(20p)
Gallon of Petrol:	4s 9d	(23p) 5p/litre
Newspapers:	5d	(2p)
To post a letter in UK:	3d	(1p)
Television licence	£5 (Black and White)	

In 1963 the standard rate of income tax was 7s 9d in the pound (39%). American Express introduced the first credit cards into Britain and freeze-dried instant coffee was first introduced by Maxwell House. Every teenager owned a transistor radio and enjoyed BBC Radio 1. Dr Who and the Daleks were born and Weight Watchers started in the US.

LIFE IN 1963 - HARDER

```
O Y J E I S F D A L E K S Y W L Q R Y R
G C H X D E S B Y R P S Y M F L H P I J
K L U P H G N E H T R A N S I S T O R L
I O V E R J E X R V M O M O V E M E N T
N G A C E U C A T P A I W C A A N Z O E
G K N T K S H T K M X X K E Y I M F T T
T E V A L B L E I F B E V P Q G F U H A
N G L N A B D M Z N Y B N R A E L C U N
E G D C W C X O M D T G D A E N S G W I
M T G Y N R J C S A N O T V C C W M T M
A I N D E A W N G I R L L S U I C A K U
N M U F V D R I N S D T A E I F R W B L
R E O I A I A I E R F H I V R N F E K L
O R Y Y R O L T W C W W R N A A I B M I
V P H C C C O H W C I A U B L L N M O A
N I O O E K O S M A N T E I V U A C E Z
X A J D H G L K W Z E M S H K F T M E F
M S I L A U D I V I D N I P L L Z H P E
L V Y R N C F E C M G C Q D O K B E E I
M R E X C I T I N G X K S X N Y E K P R
```

EXPECTANCY
INDIVIDUALISM
VIETNAM
CRAVEN WALKER
ILLUMINATE
AMERICAN EXPRESS

DECLINING
FEMINIST
INTOLERANCE
LAVA LAMP
ORNAMENT
TRANSISTOR

EXCITING
MOVEMENT
MARTIN LUTHER
EGG TIMER
INCOME TAX
BBC RADIO

YOUNG
NUCLEAR
KING
DORSET
DR WHO
DALEKS

JANUARY 1963 NEWS

IN THE NEWS

WEEK 1
    "Worst Snow for 82 Years" The Met Office forecast more blizzards to come and the West Country, already cut off from the rest of Britain by blocked roads, is threatened again.

    "Fire Cripples P&O Liner" Fire struck the 45,000-ton liner Canberra, flagship of the P&O Lines fleet, as she steamed off the southern tip of Italy.

WEEK 2
    "Electrical Trades Union Ban on Overtime" Unofficial action, in support of a pay claim, spread to the Midlands and the North. 30,000 members in the electricity supply industry were ordered to stop working overtime.

    "Move to Raise Criminal Age to 10" The Government propose to raise the age of criminal responsibility from eight years to 10 by an amendment to the Children and Young Persons Bill.

WEEK 3
    "Big Black Out in South-east" Due to "massive disconnections" of the electricity supply, and very cold weather continuing to cause rising demands for power, parts of London and the south-east were blacked out for 2-3 hours.

    "Labour Leader Hugh Gaitskell Dies" The leader of the Labour party, Hugh Gaitskell, died after a sudden deterioration in his heart condition.

WEEK 4
    "Weekend Thaw" The National Coal Board took advantage of a weekend thaw to mount a massive coal lift of 300,000 – 500,000 tons, throughout Britain.

HERE IN BRITAIN

"Snob Value Phones"

The Post Office charges 30s extra to install a coloured phone, but all phones cost £6 to make, exactly the same as the ordinary black ones which are put in free.

The Post-Master General was asked about this 'snob tax' in the Commons and told his questioner, (owner of a two-tone grey) he would "look into it"! When coloured telephones were first introduced in 1956, they cost £5 to install.

A spokesman said, "We cannot have people changing their minds about the colour on a whim or a fancy – we would have piles of black phones on the scrapheap!"

AROUND THE WORLD

"Monte Girls Crash on the Last Lap"

Ireland's champion rally driver Rosemary Smith, a Dublin dress designer, was taken to hospital in southern France with minor injuries after her Sunbeam Rapier skidded on the last lap of the toughest ever Monte Carlo Rally. Her co-driver Rosemary Sears suffered a head injury and was taken to hospital in Grenoble.

Only 101 of the 296 drivers survived the snow and ice to reach Monte Carlo in the time limit after three days and nights of nightmare driving on icy roads.

The route was littered with wrecked cars, the deadliest stretch being the final 500-miles drive the Alps from Chambery.

JANUARY 1963 - EASIER

```
S  D  R  A  Z  Z  I  L  B  R  T  R  N  C  W
T  U  O  K  C  A  L  B  J  U  K  P  D  O  E
D  T  Y  T  I  C  I  R  T  C  E  L  E  A  J
N  P  O  S  T  O  F  F  I  C  E  W  T  L  E
E  H  E  E  U  S  G  Y  R  Y  A  R  R  B  E
K  V  G  N  M  E  N  C  E  R  P  E  U  O  Y
E  H  A  O  O  Y  M  W  L  T  E  C  O  A  C
E  K  L  H  N  Q  Q  E  A  N  W  K  B  R  M
W  E  A  P  T  X  O  C  N  U  J  E  A  D  N
S  U  N  B  E  A  M  X  D  O  R  D  L  M  T
Y  D  I  S  C  O  N  N  E  C  T  I  O  N  S
F  Y  M  U  A  Z  E  M  I  T  R  E  V  O  E
D  O  I  O  R  X  X  R  T  S  F  A  N  G  L
B  M  R  Y  L  E  N  X  G  E  T  H  J  Z  R
S  S  C  I  O  J  H  Z  D  W  D  J  D  I  J
```

BLIZZARDS	WEST COUNTRY	ELECTRICITY	OVERTIME
CRIMINAL AGE	DISCONNECTIONS	BLACK OUT	LABOUR
WEEKEND	COAL BOARD	POST OFFICE	PHONES
IRELAND	SUNBEAM	MONTE CARLO	WRECKED

The Big Freeze plus the power workers 'go slow', produced unprecedented travel chaos, but there were some less publicised effects of the weather too.

Thousands of gallons of milk were thrown away on isolated dairy farms. Milk and bread was delivered by helicopter. Stranded coach passengers were rescued by helicopter. Salt stocks ran out leaving authorities with none to clear snowbound streets. The Freeze sent the price of vegetables and meat soaring. Cracks and potholes formed in roads, some over six inches deep. More than 1,500 sheep, cattle and Dartmoor ponies needed to be rescued and fed. Hexworthy on Dartmoor were without newspapers for a fortnight and Christmas holidaymakers were stranded there until the middle of January. An avalanche blocked the main railway line between Edinburgh station and Carlisle, and a shepherd and his wife were weather bound at the top of the Lammermuir Hills for 16 days. Saturday 12th was a bad day for Soccer, 41 out of 46 League games were cancelled and the Pools stopped for three weeks. Horse racing and rugby were also off. Sugar beet processing factories in Norfolk closed for lack of beets, they were still frozen in the ground.

An electricity chief pleaded *'put off Monday wash day to later in the week'* as the 'go slow' plus the Freeze caused power cuts for thousands. At Torquay and Herne Bay sea water froze. At a fire in Chester, firemen had to *start* a fire, over a frozen hydrant to get a water supply. Lifeboatmen at Walton were unable to reach their boat moored near the pier, the first time in 40 years. Lorry drivers lit small fires to thaw out their frozen diesel fuel systems. In a village in Kent, the beer froze in bottles at the White Swan and the infant's class of the school had their lessons in the Headmistress's dining room.

BIG FREEZE - HARDER

```
Y L N F Q R P Q G W T E G N E M E R I F
D K U I E Q D A I R Y F A R M D P D Z I
N E P T Y C D X A Z G B L O C K E D H V
D I U E S K Z V I A Q U S T R A N D E D
Y E C C E Z E E R F G I B C W N W E K
C Z L Q S L R Z O R A I L W A Y L I N E
G Y F L C E F R Z E R Y O X K Y T E E V
P G T H E G R P O H S F B J R S W Q G J
L F A C B C G B E O S R R G Y C O L D G
G O S L O W N L P K M D H E U H A L F M
S S H E E P I A C H F T L J S R G D J Q
K H O H R C T O C N D D R O E H A T B X
X B R W O H T Z W B B A P A O R M Z C R
K G E P A S S E N G E R S X D H A I C X
T B T W T O L A X E Y B E P F I C P L I
D E O L V H K E D M K X R A N Q J S E K
R U A F S U D H C Z I H Y R O K N T D F
T S Z B D R A N E H C N A L A V A C F F
X D E E P S N O W O U R E C C O S B Q B
Z K G A L L O N S V E Z O R F A E S L Y
```

BIG FREEZE
FRESH MILK
PASSENGERS
DARTMOOR
RAILWAY LINE
SEA FROZE

GO SLOW
DAIRY FARM
SALT STOCKS
RESCUED
SOCCER
FIREMEN

TRAVEL CHAOS
HELICOPTER
DEEP SNOW
AVALANCHE
CANCELLED
THAW OUT

GALLONS
STRANDED
SHEEP
BLOCKED
RUGBY
SCHOOL

FEBRUARY 1963

IN THE NEWS

WEEK 1 **"£4.5 million Aid Schemes for the North"** The Government provided further information about short- term construction work on roads, schools and hospitals for areas of high unemployment.

"New Blizzards Shut Roads to the West" All roads from Exeter to London were blocked again and Cornwall was completely cut off. Over 100 people were stranded in two trains in Devon.

WEEK 2 **"Queen Opens Parliament in New Zealand"** The Queen and the Duke of Edinburgh are now in New Zealand after their tours of Canada and Fiji. They will visit Australia next.

WEEK 3 **"Oyster Beds Wiped Out by Ice"** The severe weather will cause a shortage of oysters. The Kent and Essex coast produce more than half the eight million oysters eaten every year in Britain.

"£1.4m Bill for Skybolt" This is part of the cost of the cancellation by America of the Skybolt missile which was to have provided the British independent nuclear deterrent.

WEEK 4 **"Khrushchev to Withdraw Russians from Cuba"** Russia informed the United States that the several thousand troops remaining in Cuba since last year will be withdrawn by March 15.

"Tankers on Fire After Collision" Two women were among those rescued from the flame-covered water after a Panamanian tanker collided with a London tanker off Holland.

HERE IN BRITAIN

"Jet Age Spread"

The world's airlines are discovering the latest hazard of the new, fast, high-altitude jets. At 40,000 ft the falling air pressure is causing the glamorous air hostesses' clothes to become too tight. Some are finding the 'jet tummy' strain too much and slip off their tight girdles or even ask to be transferred to slower flights.

Our bodies are built to withstand a certain air pressure, when this drops, the gases in the digestive system expand causing fullness and an embarrassing increase in girth. It seems to affect hostesses most and can take up to 24 hours for their waistlines to subside.

AROUND THE WORLD

"Miss France Figures"

Muguette Fabris has found it is impossible to be the most beautiful girl in the world and continue teaching maths. Since being crowned Miss World last month, she has spent her weekends on tour, making guest appearances at casinos and music-halls but each Monday morning has been back at school.

Now she has decided to give up teaching at her high school in Angouleme for a year to concentrate on the glamour. Her Headmistress is happy about this, "*I am fed up with this beauty business,*" she said, "*with all that makeup on her face this girl should not be teaching young children.*"

FEBRUARY 1962 - EASIER

```
Y C I S S U O R O M A L G L G
A A G H P E T A G G T S D D C
G N V X I V A Q Y A E Y E A O
D A I L W I Z Y E M A S D I L
L D G E J T A L X E C T N R L
R A L E D S X O E R H E A L I
O Y V L X E C N T I I M R I S
W J Q O H G T D E C N X T N I
S G I H C I A O R A G Z S E O
S H O Y E D U N N U X H D S N
I E R I F R E K N A T C W W B
M V I S D E B R E T S Y O I L
G P J B P A R L I A M E N T W
U C O R N W A L L W Y Q F L S
D X V X Z N X W Y K N V O J I
```

EXETER	LONDON	CORNWALL	STRANDED
PARLIAMENT	CANADA	OYSTER BEDS	AMERICA
TANKER FIRE	COLLISION	AIRLINES	GLAMOROUS
DIGESTIVE	SYSTEM	MISS WORLD	TEACHING

FISHERMEN IN THE DRINK

Grimsby trawlers being unloaded

Owners of Hull's 140 trawlers are coming up to date with recruitment and training to overcome a traditional difficulty. They can no longer put the offender in the long boat until he sobers and have brought in an expert to help. *"It must be remembered that the modern trawler costs £30,000 or more and the equipment on its bridge is more highly technical than that of the Queen Elizabeth. As an industry we can no longer afford ridiculous accidents, either to the vessels or men."*

At present, men inquire for vacancies on the ships at the fish dock offices of the different firms at 9.30 every morning and deckhands, sometimes, because of the urgent need for crew, can slip by without completing seamanship courses.

In the meantime, when the trawler men return this month from three weeks or more at sea, they will receive a pamphlet spelling out the dangers of drunkenness. *"Although the days of the drunken, roughneck fisherman are long past"*, it reads, *"trouble is being caused by the small minority of men who think it is 'big' to get drunk before embarking on a trip."* Emphasizing that drinkers constituted only a handful of men, and most skippers do not mind men taking a bottle of Scotch or something with them - after all they are going off to sea for 21 to 24 days after only three days at home – it says there are still too many cases of men trying to swim ashore from ships and drowning; falling over the side; ending up in hospital badly injured – or being killed.

However, the last word comes from a disenchanted deckhand, *"You try fishing around the North Cape in bad weather. You need to be a bit drunk or a bit daft even to consider going to work in those conditions."*

FISHERMEN - HARDER

```
F S D O M V U S N Y F M Q Z G S X V C Z
O Z M J F Q N J E I F S S E C B Q G O M
D F H V M F D V S N T I C O A A N A I U
Y B F N W V E H A N P X V F D K U N Z P
Q X A T C R D N E I V V M H Q C O S C N
Y P B D O O N D D U O T U N Z R Z B E A
D A K J C S I W D E L G L U I A U P T D
E E L K G C E R E C R U I T M E N T B R
C M G R C U L A T M I O Y S E C I F F O
K R F A C F I S H E R M E N M H H G I T
H J R P T E C H N I C A L R F I O V E T
A Y D D V F W S W N F A O F Z S A L R H
N V A R F T S N O I T I D N O C H O C D
D B V N S S E N N E K N U R D P U T J R
S E R O H S A M I W S J E Z M B O N B O
R O U G H N E C K U M X G A L C R F W W
A L V S S O B E R U P P E S H Q E Z N
A G S V W P N O U M Y X W S R F R A J I
K O M V A C A N C I E S Q R S C F V C N
X D T R A W L E R S K I P P E R S T F G
```

FISHERMEN	TRAWLERS	RECRUITMENT	OFFENDER
SOBER UP	TECHNICAL	ACCIDENTS	VACANCIES
FISH DOCK	OFFICES	DECKHANDS	CREW
PAMPHLET	DRUNKENNESS	ROUGHNECK	TROUBLE
CAUSED	MINORITY	SKIPPERS	SCOTCH
OFF TO SEA	SWIM ASHORE	DROWNING	CONDITIONS

MARCH 1963

IN THE NEWS

WEEK 1   **"Pentagon Pattern of Defence"** In an important constitutional change, the Government has decided to set up a unified Ministry of Defence. This will involve the abolition of the Admiralty, the War Office and the Air Ministry.

"Waking Up to Warmth" The 6th March was the first morning of the year without frost in Britain. Temperatures rose to 17 °C (62.6 °F) and the remaining snow disappeared.

WEEK 2   **"Khrushchev Invited to Peking"** The Soviet Union and China have agreed on the need to hold a summit meeting to thrash out their ideological differences.

"Mystery of the Missing Model" Model Christine Keeler who was to have been a key witness against John Edgecombe, accused of trying to murder her, has vanished.

WEEK 3   **"New Cases of Typhoid"** This brings the total number in Britain to 24, the first ten all connected to winter sports trips to Zermatt in Switzerland.

"First Driverless Train" The first automatic trains on the London underground, now on trials, could be in operation within three weeks, the government has revealed.

WEEK 4   **"Higher Post Office Prices"** Telegrams, parcels and trunk telephone calls will all go up in a bid to bring in £14m. net extra in a full year.

HERE IN BRITAIN

"Merseyside Manufactures Motors"

To a fanfare from the Ford Motor Works band, the first motor car to be assembled 'on Merseyside by Merseysiders' a lime green Anglia, was driven off the production line and through a triumphal arch at Ford's £30m Halewood factory by the Lord Mayor of Liverpool.

The ceremony, 52 years to the day after Ford's was formed in Britain, was watched by many of the 3,000 workers at Halewood. The mayor, tactfully skirting the plant's history of more than 100 labour disputes and delays in construction, hoped the workers would realise that success depended on them adapting to new working practices.

AROUND THE WORLD

"Keeping Up With the Joneses"

Communist guards stationed at the Berlin wall had no sense of humour. 60 members of the London Welsh Choir split into two groups to travel to East Berlin where they had been invited to sing at a church. 30 went by coach via Checkpoint Charlie. 16 had the surname Jones and five were *John* Jones.

The others went by train via the Friedrichstrasse checkpoint. 14 of them were called Evans and four were *John* Evans.

The guards thought they were the victims of a big joke but were finally convinced – but they did have the last laugh, both parties were delayed for nearly two hours.

MARCH 1963 - EASIER

```
T  P  I  M  E  R  S  E  Y  S  I  D  E  X  I
B  D  J  G  G  D  T  Y  P  H  O  I  D  T  F
E  S  V  F  I  N  B  T  O  U  J  M  A  S  E
B  S  I  B  Y  U  K  Y  N  W  T  C  D  I  C
M  E  B  P  W  O  D  A  F  P  V  V  M  N  I
O  L  N  M  P  R  P  J  F  A  F  G  I  U  F
C  R  A  I  L  G  N  A  D  R  O  F  R  M  F
E  E  Y  N  F  R  B  I  K  C  R  F  A  M  O
G  V  X  O  G  E  A  S  C  E  W  H  L  O  R
D  I  N  G  P  D  P  Q  B  L  F  B  T  C  A
E  R  W  A  Q  N  T  S  T  S  R  C  Y  V  W
W  D  T  T  N  U  L  S  U  M  M  I  T  W  B
V  N  H  N  I  C  H  R  I  S  T  I  N  E  K
T  E  L  E  G  R  A  M  S  H  S  L  E  W  C
D  V  V  P  L  F  C  I  T  A  M  O  T  U  A
```

PENTAGON	**ADMIRALTY**	**WAR OFFICE**	**SUMMIT**
CHRISTINE	**EDGECOMBE**	**TYPHOID**	**DRIVERLESS**
AUTOMATIC	**UNDERGROUND**	**TELEGRAMS**	**PARCELS**
MERSEYSIDE	**FORD ANGLIA**	**COMMUNIST**	**WELSH**

WHO'S FAIR FOR FAIR ISLE?

Fair Isle

Scotland

Birds might outnumber people on Fair Isle by hundreds to one, but some of the people are rare birds too. The National Trust for Scotland, owners of Fair Isle, require unusual qualities in tenants who are offered crofts there. Apart from the ability to handle a boat, experience of clipping sheep and knowledge of wildlife are regarded as advantages for male applicants. A wife who knits also raises the points in an applicant's favour.

The island was acquired by the trust in 1954, has a population of just over 40 who make a living from sheep, crofting, lobster fishing and handcrafts, including knitting, especially the traditional island patterns, and weaving. A century ago, the population numbered 300 but 30 years ago this had dropped to 100. The Trust are maintaining the level of the population by attracting adventurous people who are not only physically fit but adaptable to the markedly communal way of life. A certain amount of capital is required by the new tenants, but they cannot buy their way into a croft, they are selected by a system which correlates their aptitude to the amount of capital they are prepared to invest.

Applicants must answer 23 questions, stating whether they have any interest or knowledge of birds or other wildlife; experience of living on an island during the winter months; if they are prepared to live in a rough climate with frequent winter gales; and other points including why they want to settle on Fair Isle. Some lose interest when they see what the questionnaire suggests is in store for them and an English woman who made corsets and who was inquiring about a croft for herself and her husband, was not, on the strength of superficial details, considered to be a wholly useful recruit for the community!

FAIR ISLE - HARDER

```
R  J  M  H  M  Q  E  Z  G  Z  N  M  H  L  W  A  C  F  S  G
L  H  S  A  W  C  V  X  A  P  T  I  T  U  D  E  Y  C  O  Q
O  R  Q  N  J  R  O  C  P  D  A  O  C  A  R  K  L  N  P  K
B  O  U  D  R  D  M  K  N  E  K  L  P  A  G  Z  N  Y  F  B
S  U  T  I  P  I  N  X  A  Q  R  T  C  C  P  U  X  G  F  J
T  G  A  C  O  N  Z  G  L  P  A  I  L  Z  D  I  N  D  L  R
E  H  P  R  P  Y  C  F  P  B  E  I  E  E  L  I  T  Q  U  E
R  B  P  A  U  P  B  T  L  P  M  L  P  N  T  J  O  A  Z  B
F  E  L  F  L  W  G  E  A  A  E  P  S  C  C  R  G  E  L  M
I  L  I  T  A  S  Y  G  T  G  O  E  A  I  V  E  J  K  K  U
S  P  C  S  T  T  U  E  N  R  E  R  D  N  R  H  H  K  N  N
H  O  A  M  I  N  H  Y  D  I  T  B  Q  N  V  I  O  Y  I  T
I  E  N  O  O  A  E  X  Y  T  T  H  M  K  X  K  A  Y  T  U
N  P  T  V  N  N  M  F  A  K  B  F  W  Q  W  V  X  F  T  O
G  O  S  N  E  E  T  C  I  C  M  P  O  Z  B  V  A  Z  I  C
Y  M  D  C  Z  T  C  K  T  L  E  N  I  R  Y  D  V  A  N  B
M  R  A  R  E  B  I  R  D  S  D  O  F  I  C  D  L  G  G  K
Y  A  W  L  A  N  U  M  M  O  C  L  S  C  O  T  L  A  N  D
T  E  I  N  G  N  I  V  A  E  W  J  I  P  Z  Q  N  I  B  O
W  I  N  T  E  R  M  O  N  T  H  S  Y  W  E  Q  J  T  F  I
```

FAIR ISLE	OUTNUMBER	RARE BIRDS	SCOTLAND
TENANTS	CROFTING	EXPERIENCE	WILDLIFE
HANDICRAFTS	LOBSTER FISHING	KNITTING	WEAVING
POPULATION	DROPPED	ATTRACTING	PEOPLE
ADAPTABLE	COMMUNAL WAY	APTITUDE	CAPITAL
APPLICANTS	WINTER MONTHS	ROUGH	CLIMATE

APRIL 1963

IN THE NEWS

WEEK 1 **"Miss Keeler to Forfeit £40"** The model who last month failed to appear in court as a prosecution witness in a shooting case, going on holiday instead, forfeited her recognisance.

WEEK 2 **"US – Soviet Telephone Link"** Mr Kennedy and Mr Khrushchev are to have a "hot line" which should reduce the risk of nuclear war being caused by accident or misunderstanding.

"Railways to be Slashed by a Quarter" The rail unions have given the Government one month to soften the impact of Dr Beeching's plan announced last month, or they will call a national rail strike.

WEEK 3 **"Anti-Nuclear Booklet Discloses Secrets"** Secret details of the system of government in the event of a nuclear attack on Britain were leaked and published by 'Spies for Peace'.

"Flexible Skirts to Make Smoother Ride" Long 'skirts' will allow Hovercraft to travel better over rough surfaces and the Isle of Wight based, Westland Aircraft, is to produce a new model, the SRN5.

WEEK 4 **"Navy Polaris Base for Scotland"** The British Polaris submarines will operate from a base at Faslane in the Gare Loch.

"Princess Alexandra of Kent Marries" Thousands of well-wishers lined the streets and millions watched on television as the Queen's cousin married The Hon. Angus Ogilvy.

HERE IN BRITAIN

"Car Park Tickets by Electronics"

An automatic ticket issuing system was introduced experimentally at one of the London Airport car parks. A car is halted at the entrance by a red and white painted barrier.

A box containing the ticket equipment is on the driver's side and a bell rings when a vehicle passes over an electronic detector.

The driver takes the ticket from the machine, stamped with date and time, and the barrier is automatically lowered when the car passes over a second detector.

When a vehicle leaves it stops at another barrier. The driver pays and the attendant presses a button raising the barrier.

AROUND THE WORLD

"They Meant it Most Sincerely"

A Russian MiG fighter fired warning shots around Hughie Green's plane as he piloted it over East Germany.

He was flying his Cessna from Stuttgart to Berlin and was over one of the recognised air corridors linking West Germany with Berlin when the MiGs suddenly appeared out of heavy cloud, one on each side, and began wagging their wings telling him to land. When he refused, one of the fighters fired several shots near his plane.

Mr Green, perfectly within the rules, maintained his course and landed safely at the RAF airfield in Berlin and the protests to Russia began.

APRIL 1963 - EASIER

```
F  D  N  O  I  T  U  C  E  S  O  R  P  W  R
S  E  Q  T  A  N  T  I  N  U  C  L  E  A  R
H  K  V  C  Q  S  T  S  E  T  O  R  P  X  H
O  I  N  N  B  A  R  R  I  E  R  A  D  Q  S
S  R  I  W  P  R  U  S  S  I  A  N  D  F  S
I  T  F  A  R  C  R  E  V  O  H  O  C  B  E
R  S  U  I  E  Z  D  J  P  Z  K  Q  W  S  N
A  L  S  R  E  T  H  G  I  F  G  I  M  S  T
L  I  Q  E  E  N  I  H  C  A  M  Q  C  E  I
O  A  W  N  M  T  L  U  D  O  O  M  S  C  W
P  R  G  N  I  K  R  A  P  J  D  O  Z  N  O
Y  N  A  M  R  E  G  T  S  A  E  J  Y  I  O
F  E  S  Y  A  W  L  I  A  R  M  R  U  R  E
Z  O  X  C  D  W  M  L  S  I  C  N  D  P  M
I  E  X  W  C  X  O  E  N  I  L  T  O  H  L
```

PROSECUTION	WITNESS	HOT LINE	RAILWAYS
RAIL STRIKE	ANTI NUCLEAR	HOVERCRAFT	POLARIS
PRINCESS	PARKING	MACHINE	BARRIER
EAST GERMANY	RUSSIAN MIG	FIGHTERS	PROTESTS

The President of the United States of America

A PROCLAMATION

Whereas

Sir Winston Churchill

a son of America though a subject of Britain, has been throughout his life a firm and steadfast friend of the American people and the American nation; and

Whereas he has freely offered his hand and his faith in days of adversity as well as triumph; and

Whereas his bravery, charity and valor, both in war and in peace, have been a flame of inspiration in freedom's darkest hour; and

Whereas his life has shown that no adversary can overcome, and no fear can deter, free men in the defense of their freedom; and

Whereas he has expressed with unsurpassed power and splendor the aspirations of peoples everywhere for dignity and freedom; and

President Kennedy presents the proclamation to Churchill's son Randolph . Sir Winston was too ill to attend.

Sir Winston Churchill was this month declared by proclamation an honorary citizen of the United States, in a ceremony at the White House. Citizen Churchill, in a letter, said that it was an honour without parallel *'which he accepted with deep gratitude and affection'*. The proclamation was read by Mr Kennedy from the steps that lead from his office to the rose garden, in the presence of Mrs. Kennedy, Mr Randolph Churchill, and his son, Winston. Mr Randolph Churchill, who read his father's letter, received the passport specially prepared for Sir Winston, the only document of its kind. The form of the ceremony was dictated by the requirements of transatlantic television and was scheduled such that this unique honour could be watched live by millions of viewers, in Britain as well at the US.

President Kennedy declared, *"We mean to honour him, but his acceptance honours us far more. No proclamation can enrich his name, the name Sir Winston Churchill is already a legend. He is the most honoured and honourable man to walk the stage of human history in the time in which we live. Whenever and wherever tyranny threatens, he has always championed liberty."*

Sir Winston now aged 88, who stirred even neutralist Americans in 1940 with his call for blood, tears, toil and sweat, watched the ceremony with Lady Churchill on television at his London home. He sat smoking a cigar whilst his son expressed the *"deep gratitude and affection"* of his father at the ceremony. The hope was that Sir Winston would respond on the satellite relay, but this was not to be. Apart from any possible indisposition on his part, the relay station at Goonhilly, Cornwall, was not ready to transmit and somebody decided against asking the French help on this very special Anglo-American occasion!

CHURCHILL - HARDER

```
X  L  Y  C  Q  S  F  N  K  N  T  S  N  A  C  I  R  E  M  A
L  D  E  C  L  A  R  E  D  T  P  T  R  O  P  S  S  A  P  A
P  P  B  O  L  Y  N  C  D  G  Y  T  L  X  U  W  D  I  I  X
M  O  C  J  G  N  N  U  S  T  A  F  F  E  C  T  I  O  N  M
I  G  U  H  E  J  O  N  R  O  S  E  G  A  R  D  E  N  I  E
L  Z  Z  D  U  S  P  E  A  S  K  C  Q  T  T  X  F  H  T  D
H  O  Y  P  Z  R  B  R  G  R  I  A  C  G  K  H  R  Q  R  U
U  O  U  A  F  I  C  B  O  X  Y  R  T  I  P  U  A  N  A  T
J  B  U  A  L  K  O  H  E  C  N  T  K  Q  O  B  L  E  N  I
A  Z  X  S  N  U  T  I  I  B  L  X  Z  N  Y  N  O  Z  S  T
K  Z  D  F  E  E  W  B  F  L  C  A  O  D  O  J  N  I  A  A
T  E  L  E  V  I  S  I  O  N  L  H  M  T  Y  V  D  T  T  R
S  E  T  A  T  S  D  E  T  I  N  U  S  A  C  A  O  I  L  G
H  I  S  T  O  R  Y  R  L  V  F  N  O  J  T  L  N  C  A  O
E  K  K  Z  N  I  A  Q  H  K  I  R  W  A  K  I  H  S  N  B
U  A  B  F  P  G  J  E  H  W  B  M  W  P  Y  N  O  U  T  D
W  D  Y  C  I  V  M  G  R  T  J  H  T  E  U  O  M  N  I  Q
L  H  I  C  W  V  V  I  E  P  I  R  Y  I  F  L  E  K  C  Y
C  S  B  G  N  U  S  X  H  T  C  E  R  E  M  O  N  Y  J  U
G  J  W  X  C  F  J  A  E  I  C  O  R  N  W  A  L  L  C  D
```

SIR WINSTON	CHURCHILL	US CITIZEN	DECLARED
PROCLAMATION	UNITED STATES	WHITE	HOUSE
GRATITUDE	AFFECTION	KENNEDY	ROSE GARDEN
TRANSATLANTIC	PASSPORT	CEREMONY	TELEVISION
HONOUR HIM	HISTORY	TYRANNY	LIBERTY
LONDON HOME	AMERICANS	CIGAR	CORNWALL

MAY 1963

IN THE NEWS

WEEK 1 **"Sir Winston Churchill to Resign"** Parliament's greatest figure of the century is to stand down as an MP at the next General Election after more than 60 of the last 63 years in the Commons.

"Hillman Imp Released" The four-seater, four-cylinder Hillman Imp is the first mass-produced British car to have a rear-mounted aluminium engine and the first car to be made in Scotland for more than 30 years.

WEEK 2 **"Rail men Call Off Their Strike"** Dr Beeching's plans will go ahead but the unions have received promises from British Railways of better terms for redundant men.

"President Kennedy Sends Troops to Birmingham, Alabama" Houses were bombed, including that of Martin Luther King's brother, in violent rioting over desegregation.

WEEK 3 **"BOAC Trap Gold Gang"** A British security officer who posed as a steward smashed an international, Pakistani gold-smuggling syndicate.

WEEK 4 **"African States Unite Against White Rule"** Leaders of 32 African nations have set up an organisation that will give them a united voice for the first time in Africa's history.

"Kenyatta to be Kenya's First Premier" Jomo Kenyatta is certain to become prime minister after his party, Kenya African Nation Union, won the country's first general election. Thousands ran through the streets of Nairobi cheering at news.

HERE IN BRITAIN

"Song and Dance at Tomato Board"

Continuing to ridicule the Tomato and Cucumber Marketing Board, Larry White, a Yorkshire grower, turned up at the annual meeting as a minstrel in pink and white trousers, bow tie and boater. To the strains of "Swanee River" he tap-danced his way up the marble stairway of Agriculture House, Knightsbridge, followed by banjo and accordion.

Mr. Wright, who is chairman of the board's publicity committee, claimed with some justification, that he attracted more free publicity for tomatoes and cucumbers than anybody else. But his performance made one producer shout angrily, "if I want black and white minstrel shows I go to Victoria Palace".

AROUND THE WORLD

"Vive Le Bingo"

Members of Shoreditch and Peckham bingo clubs went for a day out to Boulogne to celebrate the second birthday of their clubs – and what could have been more enjoyable than a couple of hours in the Casino playing bingo?

Until the French Ministry clamped down on their plan. Bingo (le loto) is banned in France, but the Brits could have played roulette, boule, baccarat or chemin de fer which *are* allowed in State licensed casinos.

Lotteries and horse racing are State monopolies. The day trippers enjoyed bingo on the plane to Le Touquet and French customs kept a sharp eye out for illegal 'bingo cards'.

MAY 1963 - EASIER

```
X  N  H  H  E  F  S  T  O  M  A  T  O  U  T
D  R  F  C  K  Y  E  D  M  T  V  D  O  F  R
G  E  B  T  I  G  T  A  M  A  B  A  L  A  J
U  D  D  I  R  S  A  M  I  N  S  T  R  E  L
Q  U  M  D  T  F  T  R  E  B  M  U  C  U  C
P  N  K  E  S  Q  S  M  U  G  G  L  I  N  G
M  D  P  R  L  M  N  U  L  A  E  H  U  G  L
I  A  N  O  I  T  A  G  E  R  G  E  S  E  D
N  N  H  H  A  A  C  W  I  E  J  L  N  B  N
A  T  P  S  R  S  I  A  O  H  I  I  W  W  Z
M  H  P  W  P  A  R  L  I  A  M  E  N  T  C
L  D  V  L  U  Q  F  Y  T  I  R  U  C  E  S
L  M  D  Y  K  K  A  I  B  O  R  I  A  N  Q
I  G  K  B  G  X  O  G  N  I  B  K  T  P  D
H  P  H  L  B  K  E  N  Y  A  T  T  A  F  Q
```

PARLIAMENT	HILLMAN IMP	RAIL STRIKE	REDUNDANT
DESEGREGATION	ALABAMA	SECURITY	SMUGGLING
AFRICAN STATES	KENYATTA	NAIROBI	TOMATO
CUCUMBER	MINSTREL	SHOREDITCH	BINGO

SPACECRAFT BACK TO EARTH

Major Gordon Cooper and his space capsule.

Major Gordon Cooper brought himself and his spacecraft down safely into the Pacific after a voyage of 34hr and 20min through space. He was forced to fire by hand the retrorockets controlling the spacecraft's re-entry to the earth's atmosphere because of a fault in the electrical system.

The capsule splashed down less than two miles from the main recovery vessel, a remarkable achievement after a flight of about 575,000 miles at more than 17,000 mph. Major Cooper was directed in the firing of his retrorockets, which slowed down the pace of his flight and brought the capsule back into the earth's atmosphere, by radio by Colonel John Glenn, the first American to orbit the earth.

The exchanges between the two men indicated that the astronaut was handling his emergency operations as coolly as he had performed all his duties throughout his day and a half in space. His Oklahoman drawl betrayed no moment of anxiety at any time during the descent.

A communications blackout happened when the Mercury spacecraft, Faith 7, had passed over Shanghai and re-entered the atmosphere but almost immediately the US aircraft carrier Kearsarge reported that it had picked up the capsule on its radar. Radio communication was quickly re-established with Major Cooper, who reported that the parachute had deployed, that all landing systems were working well, and that he himself was "doing fine". Ten minutes later the parachute and spacecraft were sighted from the deck of the aircraft carrier amid a roar of enthusiasm from the sailors lining the deck, and several helicopters took off for the point of impact to help bring the capsule on board the carrier.

SPACECRAFT - HARDER

```
K G P O P P D D R N A T M O S P H E R E
V X S R O L I A S A U I K S M L V X U A
R I Y C X Y P I A C H I E V E M E N T P
E O E T U H C A R A P I U V M G W E H B
T B E G A Y O V R P T C A P S U L E T M
R P K P Y I H O P U W R Y R T N E E R L
O J I M C V J T D G M S B S U C B J A Q
R T T A N Z P S T M A J O R C O O P E R
O F U B E Z I S H N B A B N O H S G L A
C A W S G H F W J S L Z H T N T N I S U
K R Y H R O L A E D F T U G F I M T L L
E C R A E M E L H R O O L D L C R I Z A
T E E N M S S E W B K E M L G O X Q K U
S C V G E V S G L C N M O S N E J P S Y
D A O H G N E U A N Z R B A N U C E F Y
A P C A S Y V L N O T H U T M T W I P N
H S E I L Z B M D N Y T L O F T K B G Q
E R R N Q J M S O Y L L O O C G M P O W
M E R C U R Y C P A V D E M R O F R E P
Z T C C I F I C A P P U P F E J W S V Y
```

SPACECRAFT	MAJOR COOPER	PACIFIC	VOYAGE
RETROROCKETS	CONTROLLING	REENTRY	EARTH
ATMOSPHERE	ACHIEVEMENT	RECOVERY	VESSEL
JOHN GLENN	ASTRONAUT	EMERGENCY	COOLLY
PERFORMED	HIS DUTIES	BLACKOUT	MERCURY
SHANGHAI	CAPSULE	PARACHUTE	SAILORS

JUNE 1963

IN THE NEWS

WEEK 1   **"8m Cars Out, Roads Swamped"** Whit Sunday traffic records were broken, jams put end to end would have stretched for more than 150 miles and the new M2 was paralysed.

"Pope John XXIII Dies" Just after a great sunset Mass said for him in St Peter's Square, the 81 year old Pope's brave suffering came to an end.

WEEK 2   **"Profumo Resigns Over Sex Scandal"** Secretary of State for War, John Profumo, resigns from government, admitting he lied to Parliament about his relationship with Christine Keeler.

"Ward Charged Over 'Immoral Earnings'" Dr Stephen Ward, a London osteopath and friend of Christine Keeler, key figures in the Profumo affair, has been charged with living on immoral earnings.

WEEK 3   **"Soviets Launch First Woman in to Space"** Lieutenant Valentina Tereshkova, a former textile worker, has become the first woman in space in her spaceship Vostok VI.

"Cassius Does it in Five" Although he'd been knocked down in the 4th round, the "Louisville Lip" stopped Britain's Henry Cooper in the 5th, as he'd predicted, when Henry suffered a severely cut eye.

WEEK 4   **"Warm Welcome for JFK in Ireland"** The US President received a rapturous welcome on an emotional visit to his ancestral homeland in County Wexford on the second day of his four-day trip to Ireland.

HERE IN BRITAIN

"Charles and the Cherry Brandy"

Buckingham Palace admitted the Prince of Wales did visit the bar of a Stornoway hotel and pay 2s 6d for a cherry brandy before dinner. He had gone to the Isle of Lewis on a trip round the coast of Scotland with a party from his Gordonstoun school on their training ship 'Pinta".

That evening he was taken to the Crown Hotel for a meal with four other boys – but before the meal, he nipped into the cocktail bar! Alcohol is strictly against the rules. The Prince then went with the others to see a Jayne Mansfield film – but that *was* within the rules.

AROUND THE WORLD

"Kennedy: 'Ich bin ein Berliner'"

The US President, John F Kennedy, made a ground-breaking speech in Berlin offering American solidarity to the citizens of West Germany. A crowd of 120,000 Berliners had gathered in the square outside City Hall long before he was due to arrive, and when he finally appeared on the podium, gave him an ovation of several minutes.

The president had just returned from a visit on foot to Checkpoint Charlie, where he was watched from the other side of the border by small groups of East Berliners unable even to wave because of the huge numbers of the East German People's Police.

JUNE 1963 - EASIER

```
T  M  B  H  T  A  P  O  E  T  S  O  S  Y  X
Y  R  R  S  J  P  M  L  P  W  Y  C  B  J  S
C  V  O  E  N  B  B  A  O  D  V  I  B  Z  L
A  S  A  L  E  P  R  R  P  N  L  F  J  B  P
S  P  D  R  J  C  A  O  E  A  S  F  S  C  L
S  R  S  A  R  W  N  M  J  L  T  A  X  G  J
I  O  S  H  X  E  D  M  O  E  V  R  A  H  X
U  F  W  C  J  X  Y  I  H  R  C  T  B  Q  L
S  U  A  E  N  F  Y  U  N  I  O  J  V  Z  P
S  M  M  C  J  O  Y  N  A  M  R  E  G  B  P
I  O  P  N  K  R  L  K  E  N  N  E  D  Y  M
D  C  E  I  W  D  N  A  L  E  M  O  H  A
D  T  D  R  Y  O  B  Y  G  D  R  Z  G  H  D
P  F  I  P  R  E  P  O  O  C  Y  R  N  E  H
U  V  D  U  H  F  I  R  S  T  W  O  M  A  N
```

ROADS SWAMPED	TRAFFIC	POPE JOHN	PROFUMO
OSTEOPATH	IMMORAL	FIRST WOMAN	CASSIUS
HENRY COOPER	IRELAND	HOMELAND	WEXFORD
PRINCE CHARLES	BRANDY	KENNEDY	GERMANY

INSTRUCTOR BAILS OUT

THE BRITISH SCHOOL
OF MOTORING LTD.

ESTAB. 1910.

Miss Margaret Hunter, Britain's most determined L driver brought chaos to a bustling Irish market town. She went to Lisburn, Northern Ireland, to take her third driving test in the hope, she said, of getting fairer treatment than she received in England. But again, 65-year-old Miss Hunter was failed, after successfully tying up the traffic with her blue mini. The retired schoolteacher who has struck fear into driving instructors in her hometown of Stockport, Cheshire, said, *"Everybody else seemed confused but I was as cool as a cucumber. I am very confident of my driving ability; they just don't want to give me a licence but I am determined to go on trying."*

Certainly, the Irish found Miss Hunter very trying as she drove round Lisburn with an examiner for 40 minutes. During her test she was followed by reporters, photographers, and radio and television crews. Crowds gasped as the mini, bearing four L-plates and the slogan, "Be proud of your driving ability" swung past a "No Entry" sign. Horns hooted as she pulled up behind a line of driverless taxis at the lights. The examiner explained patiently, *"You are in a taxi rank"*. There followed 10 minutes of confusion as Miss Hunter tried to back out and stalled the car seven times. Cars and lorries heading for the Ulster Motorway were at a standstill.

Miss Hunter who fluffed her first test in 1937 and her second eight months ago, failed on 12 out of 19 points. She was disappointed – just as she was the day in October last year, when on her 41st driving lesson, the instructor leapt from her car crying, "This is plain suicide. I've had enough!" He then walked off leaving her alone in her new red Fiat at the side of the A6 at Stockport.

INSTRUCTOR - HARDER

```
Z O B P X U D K G U T U O K C A B N O V
D E E F R J E R W J N B V R E T I R E D
N D R L L S T O L X E L B L I S B U R N
P E E D I K O T D U M O K C U S D J P F
G T H D C P O C E E T C W S I O Y P N T
R N C N E S H U F X A K U W L A Q G J S
N I A A N U Y R F W E Q B N D H T Y T B
Z O E L C I G T U Q R G Q E N C K X N W
B P T G E C B S L A T N N S P T W D E R
O P D N K I G N F K Q I L D W D P Y D K
I A R E G D O I N H M R E J Y N W X I J
B S G R B E I A K R G L E Q K A P C F O
L I K N N S R T E Y L R O P W L T M N N
U D B T I I I T U A F K E E O E Y C O C
E Q R H X V E P T S Y A E V C R Q Z C K
M Y O A E D I S R E S F Q N I I T A T Y
I M T P A M A R K E T T O W N R Y E M V
N I G Q O N Y B L D U Y N I O Y Z D Y R N
I B V S G C X X P A H Z N W P W T L O S
T W T F E Z S W J U B Z K X B U J Y P S
```

DRIVING	INSTRUCTOR	DETERMINED	L DRIVER
CHAOS	MARKET TOWN	LISBURN	IRELAND
TREATMENT	ENGLAND	BLUE MINI	RETIRED
TEACHER	CONFIDENT	LICENCE	REPORTERS
NO ENTRY	HOOTED	TAXI RANK	BACK OUT
STALLED	FLUFFED	DISAPPOINTED	SUICIDE

JULY 1963

IN THE NEWS

WEEK 1 **"Pope Paul VI Crowned"** A crowd of over 300,000 gathered in St Peter's Square to watch the coronation of Pope Paul VI on the steps of the Basilica.

"Harold 'Kim' Philby the Third Man" It was confirmed that the Foreign Office official who disappeared from Beirut four months ago, warned the spies Burgess and Maclean in time for them to escape to Russia.

WEEK 2 **"Britons Die in Autobahn Crash"** Six Manchester and London tourists died and many more were injured when their coach plunged over a bridge and fell 45ft to a railway line.

"Rioting in Maryland" The Governor of Mississippi said in testimony to Congress that the Kennedy brothers' civil rights legislation was sowing seeds of hate and violence that could lead to a 'bloody harvest'.

WEEK 3 **"Jackpot Order for Jet"** Britain's new BAC One-Eleven jetliner has won a £14m order from the giant American Airlines.

"Mr Khrushchev Ready for Test Ban" In a speech in Moscow, the Soviet leader said he was confident of reaching agreement with the west to ban nuclear tests.

WEEK 4 **"The Traitors' Reunion"** Harold 'Kim' Philby has been granted asylum in Russia and given Soviet citizenship. He is together again with Burgess and Maclean in Moscow.

HERE IN BRITAIN

"Horror Cards in Sweets"

The Minister of Education said he was powerless to suppress the production or distribution of picture cards enclosed in packets of chewing gum. The horror cards show scenes of bestiality as Martians invade the earth.

A set of 55 depict hideous creatures in space helmets committing gruesome acts and bear such titles as 'Destroying a dog'; 'Removing the victims' and 'Burning flesh'. On the back of the cards is a worded description.

A headmaster of a junior school who found the cards circulating among his pupils, said, *"I've never seen anything so terrifying. These cards are the vilest I have come across."*

AROUND THE WORLD

"Thousands Killed in Yugoslav Earthquake"

10,000 people were feared dead after a massive earthquake rocked the Yugoslav city of Skopje. The quake occurred in the Macedonian capital and tremors were felt some 90 miles along the Vardar valley.

More than 100,000 people were made homeless immediately as three-quarters of the city's buildings were damaged or destroyed with hundreds trapped beneath piles of rubble 100ft high. The city's hospitals soon reached breaking point and medical supplies and blood plasma ran out.

The city's main railway station was destroyed as was the post office, cutting off all communication with the outside world and the city was ringed by at least 100 blazing fires.

JULY 1963 - EASIER

```
U G R Y E N E U J A C K P O T
G W G F A Z I P S W O C S O M
Z D D N R V D S R S N D G O H
Z O G B T N S Z O T A N K H Q
M T N L H U T L T P C A F O K
W A A A Q C S N I E I L F M M
A M B W U L I C A T R Y X E A
Y M T B A E R N R E E R G L R
D F S T K A U V T R M A X E T
E K E Y E R O V K S A M K S I
H T T Y H D T S D Q Y Y F S A
S D R A C R O R R O H T I B N
N L V V C B P O P E P A U L S
U B O K B F E C N E L O I V T
J M Y S S T H G I R L I V I C
```

POPE PAUL	ST PETERS	TOURISTS DIE	MARYLAND
CIVIL RIGHTS	VIOLENCE	JACKPOT	AMERICAN
TEST BAN	NUCLEAR	TRAITORS	MOSCOW
MARTIANS	EARTHQUAKE	HORROR CARDS	HOMELESS

The Traffic Signs Committee propose that Britain's system of traffic signs should be replaced by a Continental-styled one, using mainly symbols instead of words. *"We believe"*, the committee say, *"that our existing traffic signs are seriously out-of-date in relation to the present and foreseeable numbers and speeds of vehicles".* For the ordinary motorist the most important advance under the committee's proposals will be towards clarity and away from the reading or interpretation of words and letters of varying type. The committee say that 'Halt' and 'Slow' signs should be replaced by 'Stop' and 'Give Way' - the 'Give Way' sign being mandatory and to be used on all minor roads at junctions with primary routes in rural areas.

The old signs and their new replacements

Among the new signs, 'Turn Right', 'Turn Left', and 'Keep Left' would be indicated by white arrows on blue discs. For 'No Right', 'No Left', or 'No U-turn', the committee recommend the Continental red-and-black cancelled symbol signs. 'No Entry' would be shown by a white bar on a red disc, 'No Overtaking' by the Continental two-car silhouette with a cancelled symbol and one-way traffic by a simple system of arrows.

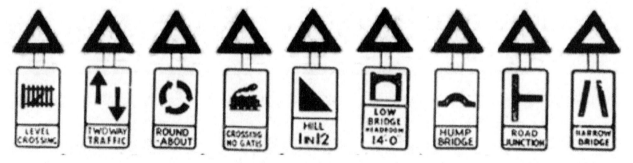

Since half the fatal or serious accidents occur at or near junctions, the committee say that minor and major roads should be very clearly distinguished by new, emphatic carriageway markings at the mouths of minor roads - a transverse, double broken white line half-way across and a longitudinal white warning line down the centre of 'the minor road'.

SIGNS - HARDER

```
U T M O T O R I S T J S G F Z R T V F T
O T R E D S Y M V E A V G Z L K X S F P
T X B R E T A D F O T U O N Q T N L E N
T G F H Y Q L L L Y C T X B I G U N N R
H S X U T W F A O A Q S V Q I K G N S J
L K J Z I H X K T A Y Y P S A I R N Q M
S U O T R I B S P N D K C B S H O A P N
G N I K A T R E V O E I K Y G I J P M B
C I N D L E V R I D F N A E T W T E L A
S H O K C A O Z U F C W I C P B C U J S
I X U E B R Z D A R E S N T F Q E E I T
D O T A P R V R E V A U Y O N D V L J N
D D U V H O T E I T J L D M I O H W K E
E N R G W W G G H T A G A S B O C E N D
R A N F U S W M T I B C C R U O E X F I
Z T U R N R I G H T C S I E E P L W L C
Y R O T A D N A M Q E L T D L A P S D C
Q F R X R T D I Q C G T E E N M S A K A
T B R I T A I N A W E W F S P I N Z R A
M I N O R R O A D S M T E B W C K E H T
```

TRAFFIC SIGNS	BRITAIN	SYMBOLS	CONTINENTAL
OUT OF DATE	VEHICLES	MOTORIST	CLARITY
GIVE WAY SIGN	MANDATORY	MINOR ROADS	JUNCTIONS
RURAL AREAS	TURN RIGHT	KEEP LEFT	INDICATED
WHITE ARROWS	BLUE DISCS	NO U TURN	RED DISC
OVERTAKING	SILHOUETTE	ACCIDENTS	MARKINGS

AUGUST 1963

IN THE NEWS

WEEK 1 **"Dr Ward Guilty – Suicide"** In the "Profumo affair", the Old Bailey jury found Stephen Ward guilty of living on immoral earnings by which time he had already taken an overdose of barbiturates.

"US Retaliation in European Chicken War" Some US tariff concessions will be withdrawn following the introduction of high Common Market duties on American chicken. US chicken sales have dropped by £16m a year.

WEEK 2 **"Chaos as Night Fire Closes Waterloo"** A small fire that was put out in 5 minutes but damaged signalling wires and points motors, cancelled many express trains and delayed thousands.

WEEK 3 **"Mail Train Robbery"** The Royal Mail train from Glasgow to Euston was stopped by armed robbers at Sears Crossing near Linslade in Buckinghamshire. It is thought up to £2.5M is stolen and it triggers the biggest detective hunt in history.

"Britain's Biggest Strike for 6 Years" On nearly 500 building sites selected by union leaders, 150,000 workers staged a week's 'guerrilla' stoppage for higher pay and a 40hr week.

WEEK 4 **"'Bus Stop' Jet is a Winner"** Britain's BAC One-Eleven made a triumphant, 28 minute, maiden flight. Two years ahead of its nearest rival in short haul passenger flying, it had won orders in excess of £50m without even taking off.

HERE IN BRITAIN

"Queen Opens Power Station"

Blaenau Ffestiniog, a slate quarry town with a population of 7,000, has always been notorious for its heavy rainfall and it was water in unlimited quantities that brought them prosperity in the form of a pumped storage hydro- electric scheme six years ago.

Heavy clouds hung over the town just before the Queen arrived to open the £15m pumped storage power station, but the sun broke through to help the 500 guests welcome her. Declaring the world's largest pumped storage power station open, the Queen said, *"Electric power is becoming more and more important, as we found out last winter."*

AROUND THE WORLD

"Unofficial Record in Three-Wheeler"

A jet engined, three-wheel car driven by American Craig Breedlove of Los Angeles, set up a new unofficial world land speed record on the Bonneville salt flats in Utah. The average speed attained by 'The Spirit of America' for two runs along the flats was 408 mph.

Under present international rules for world land speed records, John Cobb's 16-year-old record of 394.196 mph will continue to stand as 'The Spirit of America' is jet powered and has only three wheels whereas the rules state it must have at least four wheels and be propelled by at least two of the wheels.

AUGUST 1963 - EASIER

```
D  G  X  D  Z  F  L  Y  I  N  G  L  I  B  D
Y  N  V  D  Z  E  D  I  C  I  U  S  P  R  R
G  I  R  U  L  A  N  D  S  P  E  E  D  Q  O
L  D  A  D  E  T  E  C  T  I  V  E  S  E  C
U  L  W  S  S  E  D  G  Z  V  Q  V  D  W  E
A  I  N  A  U  G  A  M  E  R  I  C  A  N  R
H  U  E  L  A  A  R  T  I  E  Z  C  O  D  I
T  B  K  E  N  P  X  O  R  O  B  B  E  R  Y
R  C  C  P  E  P  H  I  G  H  E  R  P  A  Y
O  Q  I  T  A  O  X  A  K  H  A  I  N  S  O
H  G  H  L  L  T  T  U  B  E  S  O  V  V  C
S  C  C  Q  B  S  V  R  Y  X  Z  S  K  L  J
Q  S  E  T  A  R  U  T  I  B  R  A  B  O  U
T  L  L  A  F  N  I  A  R  W  K  C  X  Z  A
M  A  I  L  T  R  A  I  N  D  P  E  R  D  J
```

SUICIDE   BARBITURATES   CHICKEN WAR   AMERICAN

MAIL TRAIN   ROBBERY   DETECTIVE   BUILDING

STOPPAGE   HIGHER PAY   SHORT HAUL   FLYING

BLAENAU   RAINFALL   LAND SPEED   RECORD

MARTIN LUTHER KING

Vice President Lyndon B. Johnson and Attorney General Robert F. Kennedy with King, Benjamin Mays, and other civil rights leaders, June 22, 1963

King gave his most famous speech, "I Have a Dream", before the Lincoln Memorial during the 1963 March on Washington for Jobs and Freedom.June 22, 1963

The largest Negro demonstration for freedom since the abolition of slavery took place in Washington, peacefully. More than 200,000 came in a vast but orderly throng to the Lincoln Memorial to demand freedom now. They had come a long way since the first freedom buses were burnt by white mobs and southern policemen had turned dogs and fire hoses on them. All wore badges showing clasped black and white hands and some carried banners with the legend "Freedom in '63". Just before noon they began to march slowly down Constitution and Independence Avenues to the Lincoln Memorial. They marched about 20 abreast, to the music of brass bands, many singing "John Brown's Body" and holding picket signs with demands for freedom, jobs, housing and schools.

At the memorial, the Rev. Martin Luther King, addressed them. *"Five score years ago the great American in whose shadow we stand today signed the emancipation proclamation. . . . One hundred years later the Negro is still crippled by the manacles of segregation and the chains of discrimination. I have a dream that my four little children will one day live in a nation where they will not be judged by the colour of their skin but by the content of their character.*

I have a dream that one day every valley shall be engulfed, every hill shall be exalted and every mountain shall be made low, the rough places will be made plains and the crooked places will be made straight and the glory of the Lord shall be revealed and all flesh shall see it together. Go back to Mississippi. Go back to Alabama. Go back to Georgia, to Louisiana, and the northern slums. Go back knowing that all this will end one day. We will hew hope out of the mountain of despair. Let freedom ring."

MARTIN LUTHER - HARDER

```
L A M P Q A B O L I T I O N I S K Y X O
Z O E G F D Z B G E P N L E M U T O J P
P S M N M A I Q U E O O X I N Q O H X Y
S T O I C B M T O S O F O O M C L A Y L
R N R K W E L O N X H R I A O F U V C L
E E I R R J A H U D K T G N Y Q R E S U
N D A E W Y O M B S A R S I E O F A O F
N I L H R J T M A N S T J V A A E D U E
A S C T I V O M I N I P Y V U Y G R T C
B E O U B D A M L T A V E R O E U E H A
B R E L E R I L U B W C Q E E U Q A E E
R P H E T R H T N T F E L Y C V C M R P
A H R I C J I D F S R M E E C H A O N C
S F N S X O Y V F I R E H O S E S L W G
S V I J N D H A X X Q Z E H X L K X S S
B D A U Q Q L K R D T A V E N U E S Y
A W A S H I N G T O N N K O C Z Y C J W
N P F O G N G C I V I L R I G H T S C Q
D S O T V H H M I S S I S S I P P I E X
S A L A B A M A S M P S R L M T X H Y P
```

MARTIN	LUTHER KING	PRESIDENT	JOHNSON
CIVIL RIGHTS	FAMOUS SPEECH	ABOLITION	SLAVERY
WASHINGTON	PEACEFULLY	FREEDOM	SOUTHERN
FIRE HOSES	BANNERS	CONSTITUTION	AVENUES
BRASS BANDS	DISCRIMINATION	MEMORIAL	MANACLES
HAVE A DREAM	MISSISSIPPI	ALABAMA	GEORGIA

SEPTEMBER 1963

IN THE NEWS

WEEK 1   **"Future States of Malaysia Celebrate"** Complete independence for the state of Singapore and self-government for the colonies of North Borneo and Sarawak were proclaimed in Malaya. The four will form Malaysia.

"Christine Keeler Arrested" The "missing model" now embroiled in the Profumo affair was charged with conspiracy to obstruct the course of justice, with perjury.

WEEK 2   **"Alabama Schools Closed"** The day-old attempt to desegregate three schools in Birmingham, came to an end after a night of rioting in which one Negro was killed and the house of a Negro lawyer bombed.

"Jim Clark Wins World Championship" After a thrilling duel with John Surtees and Graham Hill, the Scottish racing ace won the Italian Grand Prix to become World Champion.

WEEK 3   **"Mob Attacks British Embassy"** Thousands of demonstrators stormed the British Embassy in Jakarta brandishing slogans denouncing the new Federation of Malaysia.

"New Year Baby" It was announced from Balmoral where she is spending a family holiday, that the Queen is expecting her fourth baby in the new year.

WEEK 4   **"Lord Denning's Verdict"** His report on the Profumo affair, criticising the PM and Ministers, sold 4,000 copies in the first hour when it went on sale at half past midnight.

HERE IN BRITAIN

"Frozen But Not Cold"

New techniques for preserving food are being developed in Aberdeen by Unilever, in order to provide better quality and a greater variety of prepacked meals. Food producers were given an opportunity to see the latest accelerated freeze-drying equipment, which does remarkable things to the most commonplace meats and vegetables.

Once the dried product is placed in water for use, it rapidly assumes its original form. Market research of certain meals compared to conventional air-dried foods is being carried out and if public reaction is favourable the production of freeze-dried foods on a commercial scale in Britain will start next year.

AROUND THE WORLD

"France May End Tourist Petrol"

There were reports in Paris that foreign motorists in France will no longer be issued with petrol coupons at a cheaper price than domestic consumers pay. If tourist coupons are abolished, it will cause great disappointment among British holidaymakers, both those travelling in France and the, many more, who regularly cross France to Spain, Switzerland and Italy.

These coupons represent a worthwhile saving on the higher cost of most grades of petrol. Premium grades vary between 6s 5d and 6s 9d a gallon, but with the coupons British tourists can buy the same for 5s 5d (27p), only a little more than the 4s 9d (23p) here at home.

SEPTEMBER - EASIER

```
M  M  O  J  W  I  E  Y  L  P  P  F  A  X  I
H  B  B  C  Y  L  B  S  J  N  S  R  Z  Y  E
B  T  P  E  G  M  Z  S  S  C  I  A  S  B  T
C  X  L  V  J  L  H  A  B  F  N  N  C  G  A
K  Z  L  R  K  H  B  B  J  P  G  C  V  N  G
A  D  L  T  U  S  L  M  C  O  A  E  D  E  E
M  M  I  N  I  S  T  E  R  S  P  X  Y  E  R
E  Q  H  P  M  M  A  D  T  H  O  A  N  U  G
N  U  M  P  E  T  R  O  L  I  R  A  D  Q  E
E  A  A  T  S  I  R  U  O  T  E  S  Y  E  S
Z  L  H  B  R  I  T  A  I  N  L  E  G  H  E
O  I  A  H  P  R  E  P  A  C  K  E  D  T  D
R  T  R  G  C  X  J  V  C  O  U  P  O  N  S
F  Y  G  H  L  A  R  O  M  L  A  B  Q  Y  D
O  K  R  A  L  C  M  I  J  H  P  W  T  S  P
```

SINGAPORE	DESEGREGATE	JIM CLARK	GRAHAM HILL
EMBASSY	BALMORAL	THE QUEEN	MINISTERS
FROZEN	QUALITY	PREPACKED	BRITAIN
FRANCE	TOURIST	PETROL	COUPONS

THE MEDWAY QUEEN

With a blast on her siren, the paddle steamer Medway Queen heaved away from the pier at Herne Bay, on the Kent bank of the Thames, for the last time this month, watched by the Mayoress and a small crowd of well-wishers. Among the 500 passengers for the final voyage were a considerable number of "regulars", one of them, a chauffeur from Highgate, has enjoyed the trip two or three times each year for the last 20 years. Medway Queen steamed at 12 knots towards Southend pier for another ceremonial farewell before returning to Strood pier near Rochester

The 316-ton steamer has plied the Thames estuary since she was built on the Clyde in 1923 and entered service on the Strood-Chatham-Southend-Herne Bay route the following year. With occasional excursions elsewhere she served on the same route until the beginning of the Second World War when she was requisitioned for the Royal Navy and converted for mine sweeping.

In 1940 HMS Medway Queen joined the 10th Mine-sweeping Flotilla based in Dover where, in May-June 1940, she played a key part in 'Operation Dynamo'. Medway Queen and her crew made seven return trips across the channel to bring the men home from Dunkirk. The ship's crew estimated that they evacuated 7,000 men while shooting down three Axis aircraft. She remained an active minesweeper until late 1943 after which she was eventually refitted and returned to civilian use with the famous Invicta motif on her funnel. In 1953, Medway Queen was included in the Coronation Naval Review at Spithead.

Her owners said that the Medway Queen's future was still in doubt, but the Paddle Steamer Preservation Society is considering launching an appeal to save the ship from being broken up.

MEDWAY QUEEN - HARDER

```
K R M E Z R I M O G A K W G W X V H H H
S M K N L L O L A N I F Q B T G K B E V
R E L O N S R Y U R R Z Z K S X Q C R E
E D G L G O O D A C I F G J P K S O N J
G W F M B Y G U E L F Q A P I V T R E P
N A J L X E B L T T N K L G T P H O B M
E Y P R O O J S E H T A P C H N A N A T
S B K E R T M U P N E I V K E P M A Y W
S B G V R E I Y Y J N N F Y A L E T O G
A W R O Q K M L X Z T A D E D B S I V L
P O C D R I E A L D N X H N R H G O P N
M I N E S U C D E A O E J C F T M N A P
L Q P W R S N S Y T P B E J A D N S D G
L M V P E F E Z U L S B D U R K M B D M
J U K R I K N U D J C D U B Q X V K L Z
A F T L E P X O M I A M I F I E O Y E P
Z E E M V O S T R O O D P I E R Y C V O
H C I V I L I A N G H A G K G C A S W G
V S E R V I C E W J B B I N K E G B B P
M G T K R E T S E H C O R F R X E K U Q
```

MEDWAY	**QUEEN**	**PADDLE**	**STEAMER**
HERNE BAY	**THAMES**	**PASSENGERS**	**FINAL**
VOYAGE	**SOUTHEND**	**STROOD PIER**	**ROCHESTER**
CLYDE	**SERVICE**	**ROYAL NAVY**	**MINES**
FLOTILLA	**DOVER**	**CHANNEL**	**DUNKIRK**
REFITTED	**CIVILIAN**	**CORONATION**	**SPITHEAD**

43

OCTOBER 1963

IN THE NEWS

WEEK 1   **"Jumping Jet Crashes"** Britain's revolutionary SC-1 vertical take-off jet plunged to the ground 20ft above Short's airfield in Belfast during a test flight. The pilot was killed.

                 "Police Appeal to 'Find Buster'" Scotland Yard believe Ronald 'Buster' Edwards wanted in connection with the Great Train Robbery is back from his trip to the Continent.

WEEK 2   **"Mr Macmillan Decides to Resign Soon"** After a successful operation in hospital, Mr Macmillan made the surprise announcement that he will step down.

WEEK 3   **"Alec Douglas Home is Prime Minister"** Mr Macmillan formally resigned and appointed *his* choice of successor, Lord Home, ahead of Mr RA 'Rab' Butler and Mr Reginald Maudling.

                 "BAC One-Eleven "Suddenly Dropped" In the second blow to British aviation this month, seven crew were killed when a 'bus stop' airliner crashed on a test flight.

WEEK 4   **"War on Stamps"** Some of Britain's biggest stores made an attack on trading stamp gift schemes. They told the housewife she is not getting something for nothing, in the end she will be the loser.

                 "Average Weekly Spend" A survey of 3,600 people revealed that we spend on average, £17 11s 11d (£17.60) per week on household expenses. It showed a fall in spending on clothes and a rise in that spent on housing.

HERE IN BRITAIN

"Police Stop 'The Adorable Idiot'"

Brigitte Bardot was stopped from filming, 'The Adorable Idiot' in London because the crowds who fought to see the blonde French star caused too much chaos in Hampstead. Brigitte will now go back to Paris to film the scenes. She said, "No more will I think Englishmen are unemotional. This sort of thing has never happened in France."

Dressed in knee length boots, corduroy tights and a grey sweater she spoke of the problems of being a 'sex symbol'. "Why do people go mad like this? Well, I admit I have a certain something – I won't say what – but I certainly have it, don't I?"

AROUND THE WORLD

"Deadly Hurricane Flora"

More than 6,000 people were killed by Hurricane Flora as it rampaged through the Caribbean in the past two weeks. The WHO has estimated that 5,000 died in Haiti, more than 1,000 were when the hurricane battered the eastern end of Cuba for five successive days. Thousands of homes, roads and railways were destroyed and crops and cattle obliterated.

Thousands of peasant families and agricultural workers lost everything they possessed. The toll of destruction and death places it on record as the deadliest storm ever to have emerged in the tropical Atlantic. surpassing that which hit Galveston, Texas, in 1900, when nearly 6,000 people were killed.

OCTOBER 1963 - EASIER

```
P  C  G  M  S  Y  P  I  C  X  U  G  N  R  K
V  D  E  A  D  L  I  E  S  T  M  J  B  F  N
M  D  N  S  X  H  U  R  R  I  C  A  N  E  P
E  E  C  X  E  T  T  I  G  I  R  B  M  L  C
M  H  A  I  C  R  A  S  H  E  S  Y  R  X  T
T  S  S  T  H  P  Z  R  A  X  N  W  O  I  O
A  A  D  I  W  V  V  R  X  V  A  P  T  A  D
Z  R  R  A  E  I  G  P  D  V  P  S  S  T  R
R  C  A  H  B  U  S  T  E  R  R  T  F  S  A
Z  J  W  D  A  E  T  S  P  M  A  H  V  P  B
L  T  D  X  E  L  B  A  R  O  D  A  V  M  Z
Y  K  E  H  S  E  Z  L  O  J  J  X  L  A  G
G  D  O  P  E  M  O  H  D  R  O  L  J  T  V
C  C  I  U  N  O  I  T  A  I  V  A  D  S  H
Y  Q  N  Y  R  E  B  B  O  R  V  Q  N  H  P
```

CRASHES	BUSTER	EDWARDS	ROBBERY
LORD HOME	AVIATION	CRASHED	STAMPS
BRIGITTE	BARDOT	ADORABLE	HAMPSTEAD
HURRICANE	HAITI	DEADLIEST	STORM

BOOMING BRITISH CAR SALES

New car orders worth nearly £100m were received at the London Motor Show on the first morning even *before* 'the official opening ceremony by Lord Hailsham'. There were crowds at every stand at Earls Court where new, 1964 models, were being presented.

In his opening address Lord Hailsham said, *"I would recommend that the customer, whether he is going to buy a political party or an automobile, to look beyond mere styling which makes a car look good, to the true design which is what fits the car for the road. The British car is a fine monument to British engineering, research, development, design and craftsmanship."*

RECORD SALES REPORTED

ROVER: So many visitors thronged the Rover company's stand to see the new 2 litre saloon that record breaking orders made it the "Star of the Show."

FORD: A total order worth £6.25m from car hire companies alone and orders for the Corsair already totalled £2.5m.

The ROOTES Group reported orders for the Hillman Minx V, Sunbeam Rapier, Husky and Singers, worth £12m plus £10m order for the rear- engine Hillman Imp.

STANDARD-TRIUMPH: Orders for the new Triumph 2000 in Britain reached £8m.

BRITISH CARS - HARDER

```
M A S B S X N E D M O T O R S H O W H Z
P S E S G A Q R M B L G P X V P I T P H
M S I X V I E Z L R O O S N H T Z N P E
I T N K R V J X T Z B O T W U H Q I H F
N E A C O J D R P A U J M A H K R K Y N
A R P R O Q N Z D W C K T I L Y S B D X
M I M X Q R I G B E Q G E E N Z E R R S
L H O I D C S E Z R V X Q S F G L E A E
L R C E I Q J A R V I E W A Q O A C D T
I A P E G V H E I Y C T L Y A M S O N O
H C M O M L C A G R X Q I O J T R R A O
I H Y B E O Q F P L P E R S P S A D T R
P K S J R N R J F M B Z L N H M C C S R
X F T D Y R F N Z X N G I S E D E T R E
P O Y Z K N O O L A S O X F Z I G N V S
S R L B O U C U C R E M O T S U C R T E
C D I N Q C B H C S X T R I U M P H N A
M E N G I N E E R I N G S I N G E R G R
Z K G N W F Z E W U D T S T O G Z X Q C
Z X B P C O A M A E B N U S C D J S F H
```

BOOMING	BRITISH	CAR SALES	MOTOR SHOW
CUSTOMER	STYLING	DESIGN	ENGINEERING
DEVELOPMENT	RESEARCH	RECORD	RECORD
ROVER	SALOON	FORD	CORSAIR
CAR HIRE	COMPANIES	ROOTES	SUNBEAM
HILLMAN IMP	SINGER	STANDARD	TRIUMPH

NOVEMBER 1963

IN THE NEWS

WEEK 1   **"Comedian to Stand Against Home"** The 'TW3'star, Willy Rushton is to stand as an independent against Sir Alec Douglas Home in the Kinross & West Perthshire by-election.

"Guy Fawkes Clashes" More than 120 revellers were arrested in Trafalgar Square after clashes with the police. Earlier, teenagers were turned back from trying to swim in the fountain outside the gates at Buckingham Palace.

WEEK 2   **"Labour Triumph Over Tories at Luton"** Ladbrokes bookmakers, after the Luton by - election, changed their odds for the General Election. Labour 7-2 on from 2-1 on, Tories 5-2 against from 6-4 against and Liberals to 250-1 against from 100-1 against.

"Swift Action Against 'Rachman' Landlords" Councils will be given new powers to curb the profiteering of bad landlords by taking multi-occupied properties into their own control.

WEEK 3   **"Kennedy shot dead in Dallas"** The President of the United States has been assassinated by a gunman in Dallas, Texas. John F Kennedy was hit in the head and throat when three shots were fired at his open-topped car.

"Johnson takes over as US president" Fifty-five-year-old Lyndon Baines Johnson was sworn in just two hours after an assassin killed President Kennedy.

WEEK 4   **"Kennedy 'assassin' murdered"** Lee Harvey Oswald, the man accused of assassinating the US President, has himself been shot dead in a Dallas police station.

HERE IN BRITAIN

"Saved in the Cabbage Patch"

A Trans-Canada DC 8 carrying 89 passengers and eight crew, ran off the runway while taking off at London Airport in fog. It came to rest in a field of cabbages where much of the aircraft's fuel was spilled, one engine caught fire, the whole plane was seriously damaged.

Luggage rained down from the fuselage but all the passengers were safely evacuated by escape chute with, miraculously, only three minor injuries.

It was soft mud that saved a worse accident but for 45 minutes the passengers wandered around the field lost in thick fog, until the fire engines, ambulances and police found them.

AROUND THE WORLD

"Wunder-von-Lengede"

On 7 November, 11 West German miners were rescued from a collapsed mine after surviving for 14 days after the Lengede Iron Mine was flooded with 500,000 cubic metres of muddy water when a sedimentation pond collapsed.

Out of 129 workers, 79 escaped during the first few hours but there seemed no hope for the remaining 50. However, on 1 November seven more men were saved after which rescue equipment was moved off-site and a memorial service for the missing men was scheduled for the 4th of November.

Then the 'Miracle of Lengede', the eleven were trapped in a dangerous, abandoned part of the mine.

NOVEMBER 1963 - EASIER

```
V S M D A L L A S J F L O H W
P R N T T A S K V F G F G A M
E E S U B L E N G E D E Y U P
C G R Y D E N N E K F E P I B
A N A P T M A O W Z K L R M J
L E G D E U C S E R L B E M T
A S L A N D L O R D S Y S M B
P S A C I B Y E L E C T I O N
R A F H Y Z R F X M D S D A N
R P A M D E P P A R T N E C I
D P R O B T R Q J J G C N W V
I S T W Z N O S N H O J T Y M
G O O B P S H L D L A W S O N
V O C A B B A G E S S H O T Z
Q O C O M E D I A N W N C A X
```

COMEDIAN   BY ELECTION   TRAFALGAR   PALACE

LANDLORDS   KENNEDY   PRESIDENT   SHOT

JOHNSON   OSWALD   DALLAS   CABBAGES

PASSENGERS   LENGEDE   TRAPPED   RESCUED

Topflight theatrical stunt men are becoming scarce as their generation ages and few good newcomers are appearing to fill the gap. Agencies' books have plenty of so-called stuntmen, but in the bar room brawls, the lower echelons mill about swapping pulled punches on the sawdust floor whilst the stunt elite smash each other through the banisters, down the stairs and out of the swing doors into the street beyond. Members of this elite now number little more than two dozen. They learnt their trade in the days between 1939 and 1945 with commandos and paratroopers showing them how to fight with bayonets and bare hands, to fall softly from heights and to drive vehicles safely at breakneck speed.

There is no upper age limit for stunt men, but many are approaching 40 and thinking of less taxing careers - directing the high diver when and where to fall rather than that of the diver himself. The qualities needed are courage, of course, but nerve, physical fitness and a sense of timing are essential. Stunt men must have brains, or they won't last very long.

With the return of the epic picture, stunts have become more demanding. The elite stuntman must now be prepared to joust at full tilt with a piano wire anchored to his back to jerk him from his horse at the moment of impact of his opponent's lance, handle a chariot and four, fling himself backwards into the sea off Scotland in the middle of a winter's night from 80ft up a ship's mast, or storm a castle wall in a rain of plastic boulders and be tossed off the ladder into the moat below. Careful planning and the liberal employment of mattresses and bales of straw reduce some of the risks of injury and death, but the dangers are still great.

STUNT MEN - HARDER

```
E S S N N K C E N K A E R B V H E P N M
M E U H O R L R G N I M O C E B J O U S T
S M O K E G Q Z T X S Y D B D N Y O S Z
X O R Y T G Y H C U F K L T V S D X Y G
E J T W K L G B S O M Q S H G F V B D E
E E C Y P I F S S C M S R E T S I N A B
L J O P L P E A Q W A M H M H L R V F R
I P U F H N A U C Y F R A N Y C Q H E E
T S P Q T B C R P Q H Q C N V W N U D V
E O Q I U L H M A F U W K E D P Z U C I
T U F J K B M X X T M F S P A O C B P D
W B N H D E L L U P R S W R J U S O O H
S R O O D G N I W S I O I C U Q C U I G
C T E Z A H D E E P S O O K B A L L B I
G O D Y V A F Q H W A G J P S W P D C H
G I A F E G A R U O C X S T E T V E C F
X R R X S T E N O Y A B L N I R N R P G
U A S Y H J W Y D Z U E F I G K S S Y B
G H J O Q K Q U A L I T I E S E W W G Q
U C E Z O H D Y K K D S T U N T M E N F
```

STUNTMEN	SHORT	SUPPLY	TOPFLIGHT
BECOMING	SCARCE	PULLED	PUNCHES
BANISTERS	SWING DOORS	ELITE	COMMANDOS
PARATROOPERS	BAYONETS	BREAKNECK	SPEED
HIGH DIVER	QUALITIES	COURAGE	FITNESS
JOUST	CHARIOT	CASTLE	BOULDERS

DECEMBER 1963

IN THE NEWS

WEEK 1 **"British Built A-Submarine Launched"** The Valiant, the Royal Navy's first all-British nuclear submarine, was named with 'Empire Wine' at the Vickers-Armstrong yard at Barrow in Furness.

"£7m Order for Concord" Orders for two Anglo-French Concord supersonic airliners, the first order from outside the United States, have been placed by Middle East Airlines, Air Liban. This brings the total of Concords on order by five airlines to 19.

WEEK 2 **"Christine Keeler in Holloway"** At the Old Bailey she was found guilty of perjury and conspiracy in the 'Lucky Gordon' case and sentenced to 9 months in prison.

"Zanzibar Gains Independence from Britain" The Duke of Edinburgh joined the celebrations and wished Zanzibar "a happy, peaceful, and prosperous future as an independent state within the Commonwealth."

"Kenya Gains Independence from Britain" The Duke of Edinburgh read a message from the Queen stating "On this momentous day Kenya takes her place among the sovereign nations of the world and I welcome her as a member of our Commonwealth."

WEEK 3 **"Britain's Baby Boom"** Figures released show that last year's record of 840,600 live births will be beaten, by at least 20,000. This is giving the Government planners a headache.

WEEK 4 **"Cruise Liner Ablaze"** The Greek liner Lakonia left Southampton on a cruise with 600 holiday makers on board. She caught fire about 100 miles north of Madeira. Passengers had to abandon ship and 24 people died and 135 were missing.

HERE IN BRITAIN
"Drinking More, Smoking Less"

The annual Customs and Excise report shows consumption of wine continued to go up in 1962/3 with a total of 22m gallons, an increase of well over 1m gallons on the standing record created in 1961, and the largest increase was in Spanish white wine.

More spirits were also drunk, up by more than 16m proof gallons which works out on average at four bottles for every adult. But the increase went to whisky and imported spirits, not to gin. Less tobacco was consumed, possibly because of the use of filter tips and reports that smoking is connected to lung cancer.

AROUND THE WORLD
"Christmas Truce"

For the first time since the building of the Berlin wall in August 1961, some west Berliners will be able to visit their relations in the eastern sector over Christmas and the New Year.

About 400,000 west Berliners, who are separated from parents, children, grandparents, grandchildren, brothers or sisters, aunts or uncles, nieces or nephews in the east, will be allowed to cross the border between 7am and midnight. More than 24,500 west Berliners filed applications on the first day the forms were issued by east Berlin postal employees. The passes are available until January 5th and valid for one day only.

DECEMBER 1963 - EASIER

```
X  E  S  M  B  N  E  W  Y  E  A  R  L  T  O
O  H  I  M  J  L  S  U  B  M  A  R  I  N  E
I  H  T  L  A  E  W  N  O  M  M  O  C  Y  B
C  R  L  S  S  G  W  Q  N  U  R  J  H  A  I
R  E  Z  S  G  N  H  P  P  A  A  X  V  W  F
U  D  H  R  N  I  I  R  R  Y  B  Z  E  O  Y
I  R  D  E  I  K  T  I  I  N  I  M  U  L  G
S  O  V  N  K  O  E  S  Z  E  Z  A  C  L  X
E  B  W  I  N  M  W  O  S  K  N  S  J  O  K
N  U  L  L  I  S  I  N  M  B  A  G  G  H  K
K  N  S  R  R  G  N  Q  S  C  Z  V  P  Z  A
Z  S  H  E  D  J  E  D  R  O  C  N  O  C  Q
Z  D  U  B  T  O  B  A  C  C  O  H  N  W  O
S  A  M  T  S  I  R  H  C  M  W  D  J  C  C
E  A  G  Z  H  B  A  O  K  J  Z  N  H  S  C
```

SUBMARINE	CONCORD	HOLLOWAY	PRISON
COMMONWEALTH	ZANZIBAR	KENYA	CRUISE
DRINKING	SMOKING	WHITE WINE	TOBACCO
CHRISTMAS	NEW YEAR	BERLINERS	BORDER

WOOLWICH ARSENAL AXED

The site of the Arsenal has been redeveloped in recent years as a new residential and cultural area.

Making artillery guns in 1897

Munition workers stacking cartridge cases in 1918

Over the next two years, the Woolwich Arsenal where armaments have been made for Britain for centuries, is to close. The long association of artillery with Woolwich began with the setting up of a gun depot there in the reign of Elizabeth 1st. Then in 1696, during the reign of William III, the 'Royal Laboratory' was established in The Warren, Tower Place, for the manufacture of ammunition and fireworks. The following year 'New Carriage Yard', where old gun carriages were repaired or scrapped, appeared and in 1716 the 'Royal Brass Foundry' was built for casting brass guns.

By the time George III paid his first visit to Woolwich in 1773, the Warren was headquarters to the 'Royal Regiment of Artillery' and the 'Royal Military Academy' as well as workshops and factories for the manufacture, proof, inspection and storage of cannon and shot. The officers came to exert considerable influence on the manufacture of guns and ammunition. George III named it the 'Royal Arsenal' in 1805 and it comprised the 'Royal Carriage Department', the 'Royal Laboratory', the proof butts and the 'Royal Brass Foundry', later the Royal Gun Factory.

The Napoleonic and Crimean Wars increased activity on the site, which expanded eastwards and by the beginning of the 20th Century, the increase in activity in the armament world, the growing complexity of weapons and in particular the serious faults in the ammunition used by the British Army in the Boer War, led to the establishment of the 'Chemical Research Department'. By then the Royal Arsenal covered 1,285 acres and stretched for three miles along the Thames, reaching its peak of production during the First World War, when it employed close to 80,000 people. During the Second World War production was distributed among other Royal Ordnance Factories nationwide, because of the risk of air attack.

WOOLWICH - HARDER

```
H Z R E S E A R C H T I A U H G P B V B
D H D Y R E L L I T R A W U I H R I M L
F V N J E G A K F D W E Z W E R J B A W
O A R S E N A L A B H C U C L Z J B A I
E O P D A P B O E R W A R H I A O U R F
L X I M B C A R R I A G E S Z R N N A Y
Y T O P E D N U G G F Y L J A Q Z A C M
R T K L A C I M E H C E A T B Y G C M E
A M M U N I T I O N C C O R E Z A S Q Z
T S G T B L W S N A A R N L T G S Z S N
I V F O R T Z J L D Y A Y W H A H T E W
L T Q I H E G P E D P H X N R W N R H P
I O X A R Q R M I O C N A B K E R A L D
M K M U U E Y K L M I E L M M A W W Y B
E E L S W C W E U A M M X A W R P I F M
S S L O N K O O T I S W M E Y K O L I U
B I T M V N G I R G H R H V U O P L G I
R K F I I I R C N K A T K G S A R I Q M
S F U C W B I Z I X S C Q S L G F A K D
P J L S W O O L W I C H U O Z M L M M T
```

WOOLWICH	**ARMAMENTS**	**BRITAIN**	**ARSENAL**
ARTILLERY	**GUN DEPOT**	**ELIZABETH**	**WILLIAM**
LABORATORY	**THE WARREN**	**TOWER PLACE**	**BRASS**
AMMUNITION	**FIREWORKS**	**CARRIAGES**	**ROYAL**
MILITARY	**ACADEMY**	**NAPOLEONIC**	**CRIMEAN**
BOER WAR	**CHEMICAL**	**RESEARCH**	**THAMES**

1960

May: Princess Margaret marries photographer, Anthony Armstrong-Jones at Westminster Abbey. It is the first royal marriage to be televised.

Nov: "Lady Chatterley's Lover" sells 200,000 copies in one day following its publication since the ban enforced in 1928 is lifted.

1961

Jan: The farthing, used since the 13th Century, ceases to be legal tender in the UK.

Apr: The US attack on "The Bay of Pigs" in Cuba was defeated within two days by Cuban forces under the direct command of their Premier, Fidel Castro.

1962

Jan: An outbreak of smallpox infects 45 and kills 19 in South Wales. 900,000 people in the region are vaccinated against the disease.

Dec: The "Big Freeze" starts in Britain. There are no frost-free nights until 5 March 1963.

1963

June: Kennedy: 'Ich bin ein Berliner' The US President Kennedy, has made a ground-breaking speech in Berlin offering American solidarity to the citizens of West Germany.

Aug: 'The Great Train Robbery' on the travelling Post Office train from Glasgow to Euston, takes place in Buckinghamshire.

1964

Mar: Radio Caroline, the 'pirate radio station' begins regular broadcasting from a ship just outside UK territorial waters off Felixstowe, Suffolk.

Oct: After thirteen years in power, the Conservatives are beaten by Labour at the General Election and Harold Wilson becomes Prime Minister.

The Tiller Girls At The London Palladium

1962: In April, the five-month-old strike by Equity, the actors' union, against the Independent television companies, ends, with actors gaining huge increases in basic pay rates.

1963: John F. Kennedy, the 35th president of the United States, was assassinated on November 22 in Dallas, Texas, while riding in a presidential motorcade. He was with his wife Jacqueline, Texas Governor John Connally, and Connally's wife Nellie when he was fatally shot from a nearby building by Lee Harvey Oswald. Governor Connally was seriously wounded in the attack. The motorcade rushed to the local hospital, where Kennedy was pronounced dead about 30 minutes after the shooting. Mr Connally recovered.

THE 60s NEWS - EASIER

```
H B V S G O P R I N C E S S H
E Y T N E D I S E R P Q H B R
N G P A P M A R G A R E T G E
I R X U O S W A L D A J U D T
L Z Y U R W P N V A S Z A L S
O B Y T I U Q E E Z S O H H N
R Y R E B B O R N I A R T O I
A B A Y O F P I G S S C I S M
C F A R T H I N G A S L F P T
O Y N A M R E G S B I P E I S
F L A U T A B S K Y N G J T E
N O S L I W D L O R A H M A W
J C K E N N E D Y E T T D L D
V C A S T R O S X D E R T M U
O O C C F U M U N D D B D X X
```

PRINCESS	MARGARET	WESTMINSTER	FARTHING
BAY OF PIGS	CASTRO	KENNEDY	GERMANY
TRAIN ROBBERY	CAROLINE	HAROLD WILSON	EQUITY
PRESIDENT	OSWALD	ASSASSINATED	HOSPITAL

1969 APOLLO 11. Neil Armstrong becomes the first man to walk on the moon. "One small step for man, one giant leap for mankind."

1965: In January, Sir Winston Churchill dies aged 90. Sir Winston served as Prime Minister of the United Kingdom from 1940-45 and again from 1951-1955. He is best known for his wartime leadership as PM.

1965

Mar: 3,500 US Marines, the first American ground combat troops arrive in Da Nang, South Vietnam.

Aug: Elizabeth Lane is appointed as the first ever female High Court Judge. She is assigned to the Family Division.

1966

Jun: The first British credit card, the Barclaycard, is introduced by Barclays. It has a monopoly in the market until the Access Card is introduced in 1972.

Sept: HMS Resolution is launched at Barrow-in-Furness. It is the first of the Polaris ballistic missile submarines, armed with 16 Polaris A missiles.

1967

Jan: Donald Campbell, the racing driver and speedboat racer, was killed on Coniston Water whilst attempting to break his own speed record.

Dec: The Anglo-French Concorde supersonic aircraft was unveiled in Toulouse, France.

1968

Jun: The National Health Service reintroduces prescription charges, abolished by the Labour Govt. in 1965, at 2s 6d.

Sep: The General Post Office divides their single rate postal service into two. First-class letters at 5d and second-class at 4d.

1969

Mar: The Queen opens the Victoria Line on the London Underground. It is the first entirely new Underground line in London for 50 years.

Dec: The abolition of the death penalty for murder, having been suspended since 1965, was made permanent by Parliament.

The 60s News - Harder

```
T D Q V S U E X Y N P O L A R I S Y Q L
T N Z X P N S R D S W K N A E X W L N T
V U Q N O P V M D B U W O R R A B U E H
I O Y D D H R S A T F S D C I E D N G K
R R J R R Z O E D R H B P N H H A N C D
E G L O A T Y R I V I X A M H L O O S I
N R Q C C G T V S L T N S F H R N Q Y P
I E Z E Y K A I Z A Z R E T T I D N M R
R D V R A A B C Q T E N E S S T I W B E
A N X S L M M E V S B B M T A F K F I S
M U W W C K O E O K A R O O V Z I W F C
B M I Q R D C L H Z A N B U X Z D K O R
U O N I A L U N I O E D G N F K Z S K I
S N S Z B T X L E Z E N A C I R E M A P
E O T W I W E K K E E D R O C N O C D T
C P O O F W A O P M A N T E I V N N S I
H O N R F K O S K O T O V J O H U U T O
F L X N K R V I C T O R I A L I N E F N
F Y Q A C C E S S E C I F F O T S O P R
W E R K K L L E B P M A C D L A N O D W
```

US MARINES	AMERICAN	COMBAT	VIETNAM
ELIZABETH LANE	BARCLAYCARD	MONOPOLY	ACCESS
HMS RESOLUTION	BARROW	SUBMARINE	POLARIS
DONALD CAMPBELL	SPEEDBOAT	CONISTON	RECORD
CONCORDE	PRESCRIPTION	POST OFFICE	SERVICE
VICTORIA LINE	UNDERGROUND	ARMSTRONG	WINSTON

At the beginning of the decade, the wireless was still the usual form of entertainment in the home and children could sit comfortably to "Listen with Mother" on the Light Programme and mother could carry on listening to "Woman's Hour" afterwards.

However, television was becoming increasingly affordable, and the two channels, BBC and ITV were joined in 1965 by BBC2. Dr Finlay's Casebook; The Black and White Minstrel Show; Top of the Pops; Perry Mason and Z Cars were the most popular shows of the 60's.

In 1962 the BBC bravely introduced a new satirical show, "That Was the Week That Was" which proved a big hit and by 1969, the BBC was converting programmes to colour.

Children's pocket money, probably 6d (2.5p) a week in the early years, could buy sweets. Black Jacks and Fruit Salads (4 for a penny (0.5p)), sweet cigarettes, lemonade crystals, gob stoppers, flying saucers or toffees, weighed by the shopkeeper in 2oz or 4oz paper bags. All could be eaten whilst reading a copy of The Beano or Dandy, Bunty or Jack and Jill comics.

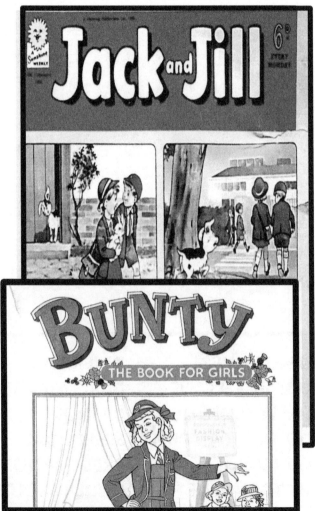

The simple, yet addictive party game Twister was introduced in 1966.

THE 60s HOME - EASIER

```
M  J  R  Y  S  S  E  L  E  R  I  W  H  X  T
N  H  B  N  M  T  T  W  I  S  T  E  R  U  Y
B  Y  E  A  P  E  I  J  C  O  L  O  U  R  C
F  L  A  D  A  P  E  R  R  Y  M  A  S  O  N
F  E  N  A  G  T  Z  F  G  C  J  O  L  W  T
C  R  O  L  B  O  C  W  R  H  O  H  A  O  L
A  T  Y  A  L  E  A  O  A  I  P  J  C  M  W
S  S  K  S  F  A  R  P  W  L  J  D  I  A  A
E  N  K  T  A  N  S  D  Z  D  R  G  R  N  N
B  I  E  I  V  D  I  S  X  R  R  X  I  S  G
O  M  R  U  V  S  D  P  P  E  R  Q  T  H  X
O  Z  Q  R  X  O  Q  R  P  N  G  M  A  O  D
K  E  W  F  V  N  W  K  Q  D  W  T  S  U  X
Q  Y  D  N  A  D  R  F  I  N  L  A  Y  R  U
F  U  L  K  L  L  I  J  D  N  A  K  C  A  J
```

STEPTOE AND SON	FRUIT SALADS	BEANO	DANDY
JACK AND JILL	TWISTER	WIRELESS	CHILDREN
WOMANS HOUR	DR FINLAY	CASEBOOK	MINSTREL
PERRY MASON	Z CARS	SATIRICAL	COLOUR

In the 60's the nuclear family was still the norm, father out at work and mother busy with the housework which was time consuming before the general possession of electrical labour-saving devices.

Washing up was done by hand and laundry gradually moved to machines over the decade.

Twin tubs, one for washing and one for Spinning, became popular in the late 60's and were usually wheeled into the kitchen to be attached to the cold tap and afterwards, have the waste-water emptied into the sink. The 'housewife' had to be at home to transfer the wet washing from the washing tub to the spinning tub.

By the end of the 60's, 58% of households had a small refrigerator but no fridge/freezers, so shopping was still done regularly and, typically, meals were home cooked.

Chicken was expensive but beef was cheaper and olive oil came only in tiny bottles from the chemist to help clean your ears!

In Britain, the domestic freezer is still a luxury but by the mid 60's, some 700m fish fingers were among the 60,000 tons of frozen fish consumed with peas from 35,000 acres and 120,000 quick-frozen chickens.

Goods came to you. The milkman delivered the milk to your doorstep, the baker brought the baskets of bread to the door, the greengrocer delivered and the 'pop man' came once a week with 'dandelion and burdock', 'cherryade' or 'cream soda' and the rag and bone man called down the street for your recycling.

THE 60s HOME - HARDER

```
J N A M K L I M L X M P R F X X A U H K
S R A E L C U N F Z K A V B X A K V E Y
C T R E F R I G E R A T O R F P M A O W
N N B Q G A D R M Q X Y U Y F O A V U H
F H W V R J C H E M I S T I U B X L H L
U O W I H E G M A E B B S T R M M A S A
V U A H Y L T B K A T H Q I X R U B P C
H S S O R K M A P W F J T F R B U O D I
Z E H U D K I Q W I N A R O D T X U B R
U W I S N J X T N E I X O P N F O R D T
U O N E U M L G C N T Q H I O C T S F C
B R G W A R E I Z H F S W X N Q C A A E
W K U I L R Y X O L E T A R L T H V M L
W N P F S O T V G E F N C W Z Z I I I E
M Q U E Q K H W U E V U B L O A C N L V
Z R E Z E E R F E G D I R F G Q K G Y E
R D O M E S T I C S S E L P G E E Q J E
S O F R O Z E N G N I P P O H S N Z U H
B H K J O E K L N J B I R D S E Y E H R
G K R P T V A T Q O N O I L E D N A D Z
```

BIRDS EYE	HOUSEWORK	NUCLEAR	FAMILY
LABOUR SAVING	ELECTRICAL	WASHING UP	LAUNDRY
TWIN TUBS	WASTE WATER	HOUSEWIFE	KITCHEN
FRIDGE FREEZER	REFRIGERATOR	SHOPPING	CHICKEN
OLIVE OIL	CHEMIST	DOMESTIC	BRITAIN
FISH FINGERS	FROZEN	DANDELION	MILKMAN

1960 - 1963

1960 Frederick Ashton's 'La Fille Mal Gardée' premieres by The Royal Ballet at the Royal Opera House.
In court, Penguin Books who published 'Lady Chatterley's Lover' by DH Lawrence, is found not guilty of obscenity.

1961 The 'Betting & Gaming Act' comes into force which allows the operating of commercial Bingo halls.
'Ken' is introduced in the US as a boyfriend for 'Barbie'.

1962 Margot Fonteyn and Rudolf Nureyev first dance together in a Royal Ballet performance of Giselle, in London.
Dec John Steinbeck, American author is awarded the Nobel Prize in Literature. Aleksandr Solzhenitsyn's novella, "One Day in the Life of Ivan Denisovich" is published in Russia.

1963 The first Leeds Piano Competition is held, and Michael Roll is the winner.
Authors CS Lewis and Aldous Huxley both die on 23 November, but news of their deaths is overshadowed by the assassination of JFK.

Margot Fonteyn and Rudolf Nureyev performing The Sleeping Beauty.

Their partnership has been described as the greatest of all time.

1964 - 1969

1964 BBC television airs the first 'Top of the Pops'. Dusty Springfield is the very first artist to perform, with 'I Only Want to Be With You'.
Ernest Hemingway's memoirs of his years in Paris, 'A Moveable Feast' is published posthumously by his wife.

1965 Rembrandt's painting 'Titus' is sold at Christie's London fetching the then record price of 760,000 guineas. (£798,000).
The f*** word is spoken for the first time on television by Kenneth Tynan and two weeks later, Mary Whitehouse founds The National Viewers' and Listeners' Association.

1966 'Rosencrantz and Guildenstern Are Dead' by Tom Stoppard has its debut at the Edinburgh Festival Fringe.
BBC1 televises 'Cathy Come Home', a docudrama that is viewed by a quarter of the British public and goes on to influence attitudes to homelessness.

1967 **'The Summer of Love'.** Thousands of young 'flower children' descend on the west coast of America, for hippie music, hallucinogenic drugs, spiritual meditation and free-love.
BBC radio restructures. The Home Service becomes Radio 4, the Third Programme becomes Radio 3 and the Light Programme is split between Radio 1 (to compete with pirate radio) and Radio 2.

1968 The BBC repeat of the twenty-six episodes of 'The Forsyte Saga' on Sunday evening television, leads to reports of 'publicans and vicars complaining it was driving away their customers and worshippers, respectively' and of 'Evensong services being moved to avoid a clash'.

1969 The Beatles perform together for the last time on the rooftop of Apple Records in London. The impromptu concert was broken up by the police.

ART AND CULTURE - EASIER

```
H A L L U C I N O G E N I C V
E S U O H A R E P O L A Y O R
I Y T X Y B Y J O M P Y F D M
M E D R A P P O T S R Q O V S
Z V N Z T D N A R B M E R L D
G G K S I W E L S C U O S P W
B D L E I F G N I R P S Y E H
Z G S N B E A T L E S D T U I
O N Z Y Y I Y X C O N C E R T
E F P T B P W C U Z H E S M E
T E L L A B T S E N R E A N H
L E E D S P I A N O O I G N O
N G F I N L Y H T A C C A O U
U G T L L A H O G N I B V Y S
W S R C H A T T E R L E Y H E
```

ROYAL OPERA HOUSE   CHATTERLEY   BINGO HALL   BALLET

LEEDS PIANO   CS LEWIS   SPRINGFIELD   ERNEST

REMBRANDT   WHITEHOUSE   STOPPARD   CATHY

HALLUCINOGENIC   FORSYTE SAGA   BEATLES   CONCERT

The three-day Woodstock Music Festival was held in August 1969 on a dairy farm in Bethel, New York. Nearly half a million young people arrived for "An Aquarian Experience: 3 Days of Peace and Music." Now known simply as Woodstock, the festival was a huge success, but it did not go off without a hitch. The almost 500,000 people who turned up was unexpected and caused the organisers a headache which necessitated venue changes and this was before the bad weather, muddy conditions, lack of food and unsanitary conditions made life even more difficult.

Surprisingly, the event passed off peacefully, this fact attributed by most, to the amount of sex, psychedelic drugs and rock 'n roll that took place. Others say, couples were too busy 'making love not war' to cause trouble, either way, Woodstock earned its place in the halls of pop culture history fame.

"American artist Andy Warhol premieres his "Campbell's Soup Cans" exhibit in Los Angeles".

Andy Warhol famously borrowed familiar icons from everyday life and the media, among them celebrity and tabloid news photos, comic strips, and, in this work, the popular canned soup made by the Campbell's Soup Company. When he first exhibited "Campbell's Soup Cans", the images were displayed together on shelves, like products in a grocery aisle. At the time, Campbell's sold 32 soup varieties and each one of Warhol's 32 canvases corresponds to a different flavour, each having a different label. The first flavour, introduced in 1897, was tomato.

Each canvas was hand painted and the fleur de lys pattern round each can's bottom edge was hand stamped. Warhol said, "I used to drink Campbell's Soup. I used to have the same lunch every day, for 20 years, I guess!"

ART AND CULTURE - HARDER

```
L V P R V K S S O F C K R O Y W E N A D
W D G O R S U N S A N I T A R Y G M A Y
N X Z C O P E J T F U C T E H Y F V I V
P U H K J O A N A T N A S I S J I M F C
E B L A L T A S U R P R I S I N G L Y N
A A B N D Y U A B B E D P M O R D W W G
C D A D X D L Q E H N I I D S T F J J R
E W G R C D E G Q K E H I R H G R K O X
F E L O M U S I C F E S T I V A L C E G
U A O L U M O N M N Z T W W Q I H O C B
L T V L W D C J D A A C U H M H S T O S
L H E K C P A R T E N R A D A O G S C Q
Y E N Y I O I Q H O V D A M U R B D K S
T R O N P X U D U Q M T Y P P U T O E N
H B T R B M E P L A X A C W J B Y O R O
E F W U L N O R L X R A T D A R E W X C
W Z A D N L J S U E N I I O P R I L M I
H D R A Y M Q L S S S O A X D V H V L F
O X C H L Y A D Y R E V E N D B U O O U
A P S Y C H E D E L I C M Y E X P D L C
```

WOODSTOCK   **MUSIC FESTIVAL**   **NEW YORK**   **AQUARIAN**
JIMI HENDRIX   **CANNED HEAT**   **SANTANA**   **THE WHO**
JOE COCKER   **BAD WEATHER**   **UNSANITARY**   **MUDDY**
SURPRISINGLY   **PEACEFULLY**   **PSYCHEDELIC**   **COUPLES**
ROCK AND ROLL   **LOVE NOT WAR**   **EVERYDAY**   **ICONS**
ANDY WARHOL   **SOUP CANS**   **CAMPBELL**   **TOMATO**

FILMS IN THE 60s - 1

1960 - 1963

1960 **Ben Hur**, the religious epic, was a remake of a 1925 silent film with a similar title and had the largest budget ($15.175m) and the largest sets built of any film produced at the time.

1961 Billy Wilder's risqué tragi-comedy **The Apartment** won the Academy Award for Best Picture. Starring Jack Lemmon and Shirley MacLaine, it tells a story of an ambitious, lonely insurance clerk who lends out his New York apartment to executives for their love affairs.

1962 New Films released this year included, **Lolita** starring James Mason and Sue Lyon. **Dr No**, the first James Bond film, starring Sean Connery and Ursula Andress and **What Ever Happened to Baby Jane?** a horror film with Bette Davis

1963 **Lawrence of Arabia**, based on author TS Eliot's book 'Seven Pillars of Wisdom' and starring Peter O'Toole and Alec Guinness won the Oscar for Best Picture.
The publicity of the affair between the stars, Elizabeth Taylor and Richard Burton, helped make **Cleopatra** a huge box office success but the enormous production costs, caused the film to be a financial disaster.

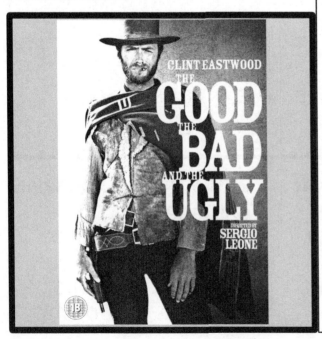

1964 - 1969

1964 The historical adventure, sex comedy romp **Tom Jones** won four Oscars, Best Picture, Best Director, Best Adapted Screenplay and Best Musical Score. Albert Finney starred as the titular hero and Susannah York as the girl he loves.

1965 Winning the Oscar this year, the film **My Fair Lady,** based on George Bernard Shaw's play 'Pygmalion', tells the story of Eliza Doolittle and her quest to 'speak proper' in order to be presentable in Edwardian London's high society. Rex Harrison and Audrey Hepburn starred and it became the 2nd highest grossing film of the year just behind **The Sound of Music** which won the Academy Award the following year.

1966 **The Good, the Bad and the Ugly** was directed by Sergio Leonie, the Italian director who gave rise to the term 'spaghetti western'- a genre of westerns produced and directed by Italians. Clint Eastwood was the Good, Lee Van Cleef, the Bad and Eli Wallach, the Ugly. The film was a huge success and catapulted Clint Eastwood to fame.

1967 The fun filled seduction of Benjamin Braddock by Mrs Robinson in **The Graduate** made the film the biggest grossing production of the year world-wide.

1968 The famous quote "They call me Mister Tibbs" comes from **In the Heat of the Night** where Sidney Poitier plays Virgil Tibbs, a black police detective from Philadelphia, caught up in a murder investigation in racially hostile Mississippi. Rod Steiger is the white chief of police.

1969 **Oliver** the musical based on Dicken's novel and Lionel Bart's stage show, carried off the Oscar for Best Picture.

Editor's Note: The Academy Awards are held in February and each year's awards are presented for films that were first shown during the full preceding calendar year from January 1 to December 31 Los Angelis, California. Source: Wikipedia

FILMS IN THE 60s - EASIER

```
L Y U D O O W T S A E E N R W
O D P P E T E R O T O O L E Q
L A A G E H O L I V E R A E V
I L B V R C D I K L T P B T R
T R A I U J M R X F O S E A E
A I B R T A A T W X M O N U G
W A Y G C C R F Y D J S H D I
H F J I I K T P N P O C U A E
F Y A L P L A I R F N A R R T
R M N T T E P L A U E R T G S
W F E I S M O B U Z S A A E W
T G B B E M E Y U J O Y S H S
R X G B B O L X W P O R S T O
I B F S L N C J R Y L V K C A
Y T N I L C G B T U O O X G U
```

BEN HUR	**JACK LEMMON**	**LOLITA**	**BABY JANE**
PETER O TOOLE	**BEST PICTURE**	**CLEOPATRA**	**OSCAR**
TOM JONES	**MY FAIR LADY**	**EASTWOOD**	**CLINT**
THE GRADUATE	**VIRGIL TIBBS**	**STEIGER**	**OLIVER**

THE FIRST JAMES BOND FILM!

HARRY SALTZMAN and ALBERT R. BROCCOLI PRESENT IAN FLEMING'S **DR. NO** TECHNICOLOR **SEAN CONNERY** AS 007 URSULA **ANDRESS** · JOSEPH **WISEMAN** · JACK LOI

Screenplay by RICHARD MAIBAUM JOHANNA HARWOOD BERKELY MATHER Directed by TERENCE YOUNG Produced HARRY SALT.

This was the first-ever launch of a James Bond film in a cinema and was attended by the stars, Sean Connery and Ursula Andress together with the James Bond creator Ian Fleming. The plot of this British spy film revolves around James Bond who needs to solve the mystery of the strange disappearance of a British agent to Jamaica and finds an underground base belonging to Dr No who is plotting to disrupt the American space launch with a radio beam weapon. The film was condemned by The Vatican as "a dangerous mixture of violence, vulgarity, sadism, and sex".

1962 : "West Side Story" Wins The Academy Awards "Best Picture" category.

The musical with lyrics by Stephen Sondheim and music by Leonard Bernstein was inspired by the story of William Shakespeare's "Romeo and Juliet". Set in the mid 1950s in Upper West Side of New York City, which was then, a cosmopolitan working-class area, it follows the rivalry between the Jets and the Sharks, two teenage street gangs from different ethnic backgrounds.

The Sharks are from Puerto Rico and are taunted by the white Jets gang. The hero, Tony, a former member of the Jets falls in love with Maria, the sister of the leader of the Sharks. The sophisticated music and the extended dance scenes, focussing on the social problems marked a turning point in musical theatre. The film starred Natalie Wood and Richard Beymer.

MIRISCH PICTURES presents A ROBERT WISE PRODUCTION

WEST SIDE STORY

NATALIE WOOD
RICHARD BEYMER
RUSS TAMBLYN
RITA MORENO
GEORGE CHAKIRIS

Produced ROBERT WISE Directed JEROME ROBBINS Screenplay ERNEST LEHMAN Music LEONARD BERNSTEIN Lyrics STEPHEN SONDHEIM ROBERT E. GRIFFITH HAROLD S. PRINCE JEROME ROBBINS ARTHUR LAURENTS

UNITED ARTISTS

FILMS IN THE 60s - HARDER

```
B  I  C  R  A  D  I  O  B  E  A  M  Z  M  J  H  U  D  M  S
H  I  A  N  F  L  E  M  I  N  G  W  E  I  A  H  N  E  Y  O
C  P  T  M  Z  W  D  N  S  E  A  C  N  Y  M  A  D  N  D  F
N  U  A  W  L  S  M  Z  S  N  N  O  S  T  A  L  E  M  R  T
U  C  Q  B  U  M  Q  N  E  A  A  I  B  I  I  O  R  E  D  I
A  Y  E  Y  W  G  S  U  R  F  N  G  O  C  C  R  G  D  C  H
L  R  R  S  Y  H  X  A  D  S  B  B  E  K  A  E  R  N  O  S
E  A  L  E  A  L  E  X  N  P  V  R  A  R  Z  V  O  O  S  I
C  Q  C  R  N  P  A  Z  A  Y  D  I  M  O  J  V  U  C  M  E
A  I  K  A  P  N  E  C  A  F  P  T  E  Y  A  R  N  E  O  C
P  S  P  A  D  G  O  G  L  I  C  I  R  W  S  Z  D  R  P  N
S  X  S  T  N  E  I  C  U  L  Y  S  I  E  W  J  J  U  O  E
F  I  R  A  E  Q  M  E  S  M  Q  H  C  N  W  A  E  T  L  L
D  T  R  B  I  T  B  Y  R  C  L  W  A  K  V  M  X  C  I  O
P  T  C  D  L  A  X  V  U  E  S  T  N  N  X  E  Q  I  T  I
S  W  E  S  T  S  I  D  E  S  T  O  R  Y  Z  S  W  P  A  V
D  F  V  T  T  H  B  F  M  O  G  C  G  O  B  H  W  N  R
W  Z  T  H  E  V  A  T  I  C  A  N  O  P  N  O  H  B  W  P
Z  A  D  N  U  D  V  J  N  A  F  D  R  K  P  N  Q  S  T  L
H  M  U  S  I  C  A  L  A  F  G  P  U  D  Q  D  J  Z  S  H
```

JAMES BOND	IAN FLEMING	CONNERY	DR NO
URSULA ANDRESS	SPY FILM	BRITISH	STRANGE
DISAPPEARANCE	UNDERGROUND	JAMAICA	AMERICAN
SPACE LAUNCH	RADIO BEAM	THE VATICAN	VIOLENCE
CONDEMNED	WEST SIDE STORY	ACADEMY	PICTURE
NEW YORK CITY	COSMOPOLITAN	SHARKS	MUSICAL

FASHION IN THE 60s - 1

CHANGING FASHION

It was a decade of three parts for fashion. The first years were reminiscent of the fifties, conservative and restrained, classic in style and design. Jackie Kennedy, the President's glamorous wife, was very influential with her tailored suit dresses and pill box hats, white pearls and kitten heels.

The hairdresser was of extreme importance. Beehive coiffures worn by the likes of Dusty Springfield and Brigitte Bardot were imitated by women of all ages and Audrey Hepburn popularised the high bosom, sleeveless dress. Whilst low, square toed shoes were high fashion, 'on the street', stilettos rivalled them.

THE MODS

In the mid-60s, the look had become sleeker and more modern. The lines were form-fitting but didn't try to accentuate curves. There were brighter colours and for the young, the Mod style.

Male mods took on a smooth, sophisticated look that included tailor-made suits with narrow lapels, thin ties, button-down collar shirts and wool jumpers.

The pea coat and Chelsea boots looked very 'London'. The Beatles were leading the way, hair started to grow longer, and trousers lost the baggy, comfortable fit of the 1950's.

For girls, shift dresses and mini skirts became shorter and shorter, worn with flat shoes or 'go go boots', short hair with eyebrow brushing fringes, and little makeup, just a pale lipstick and false eyelashes.

Slender models like Jean Shrimpton and Twiggy exemplified the look and new, exciting designers emerged such as Mary Quant. Television shows like 'Ready Steady Go!' showed their audiences at home, what they should be wearing.

```
Z C K E T T I G I R B S T I O
X H T P E A R L S R W P A I A
G A H B N V K X Q E X R I Z K
S N E O Y J N Z S Z D I L S N
T G B A E S L E H C M N O Q R
R I E K E N N E D Y W G R A U
I N A T M I J K X G P F M Q B
K G T R E S S E R D R I A H P
S F L B R T X I X O A E D H E
I A E J V G C I T F E L E D H
N S S D O M E H T L W D S C Q
I H J W M A R Y Q U A N T Y Q
M I O Y G G I W T J Z U N G E
Q O S O P H I S T I C A T E D
A N S P F L S U O R O M A L G
```

CHANGING FASHION	GLAMOROUS	KENNEDY	PEARLS
HAIRDRESSER	SPRINGFIELD	BRIGITTE	HEPBURN
SOPHISTICATED	TAILOR MADE	THE MODS	CHELSEA
THE BEATLES	MINI SKIRTS	MARY QUANT	TWIGGY

THE HIPPIES

For the young, jeans were becoming ubiquitous both for men and women, skin-tight drainpipes through to the flared bottoms of the late years. London had taken over from Paris to become the fashion centre of the world and in contrast to the beginning of the decade, the end was the exact opposite.

Bright, swirling colours. Psychedelic, tie-dye shirts, long hair and beards were commonplace. Individualism was the word and mini skirts were worn alongside brightly coloured and patterned tunics with flowing long skirts.

CARNABY STREET

By 1967, Carnaby Street was popular with followers of the mod and hippie styles. Many fashion designers, such as Mary Quant, Lord John and Irvine Sellars, had premises there, and underground music bars, such as the Roaring Twenties, opened in the surrounding streets.

Bands such as the Small Faces, The Who and The Rolling Stones appeared in the area, to work at the legendary Marquee Club round the corner in Wardour Street, to shop, and to socialise. The Street became one of the coolest destinations associated with 1960s Swinging London.

60s Fashion - Harder

```
N X Y Z J J Q L Q L P J N D X P G S G L
F X C B P A O C O Z A M R L Z A P C P K
S I W D S N F N G M R A U I A R B V E R
C D Y U D T G A O X I A M A A B R A Y U
A M G O A H V D L N S L O R D J O H N O
R U N Z A K S O P K M M B M C A G S B D
N S I I D B R I G H T C L O E P V M E R
A E R H B I P H X I X Y L Y M U S I C A
B N C P U E F A S H I O N C E N T R E W
Y O U O S J P H B E U H U J T I E D Y E
S T Q W X S Q I R I B H K H R B L P D
T S S N Z I Y I E P T P Q H O T M A A M
R G R I I Z C D A J P Z P A B F U W V X
E N E T F W H W C Z A I R I O N U X Z O
E I N I L L E X L M G I E F H C D N W T
T L G O A E D Z D F N Y O S B E A C P H
M L I P R B E K Z G P I W B Z V H R C E
K O S K E S L S K I N T I G H T F T B W
N R E R D H I D N U O R G R E D N U L H
P S D A A Z C I N S M A L L F A C E S O
```

THE HIPPIES	DRAINPIPES	SKIN TIGHT	FLARED
FASHION CENTRE	LONDON	PARIS	BRIGHT
PSYCHEDELIC	TIE DYE	LONG HAIR	COLOURED
CARNABY STREET	HIPPIES	DESIGNERS	MODS
LORD JOHN	ROARING	UNDERGROUND	MUSIC
SMALL FACES	THE WHO	ROLLING STONES	WARDOUR

LEISURE IN THE 60s - 1

THE PACKAGE HOLIDAY

By the mid-sixties, the traditional British seaside holiday, sandcastles, donkey rides, sticks of rock and fish and chips on the beach was gradually giving way to the new and exciting Package Holiday in the sun.

Tour operators began taking plane loads of holidaymakers abroad, almost exclusively to Europe and to Spain in particular. Hotels were springing up everywhere, often obscuring the 'exotic views' that the tourists were promised and were basic with rather simple local fare, which even then was not to the taste of a large majority. Restaurants flourished with 'Full English Breakfast' posters displayed all over the windows, tea and beer were in demand.

By the end of the decade, Luton Airport, a favourite with the tour firms, had flights arriving back every hour full of sunburnt Brits wearing sombreros and clutching Spanish donkeys and maracas.

A cold British beach holiday was replaced for many by cheap package holidays to sunny Spain.

"LET'S GO FOR A CHINESE"

A 'Greasy Spoon'
A cheese-pineapple hedgehog

In the early 1960s, eating out was expensive and apart from 'greasy spoon' cafes, or a packet of salted crisps at a pub, dining out was limited to formal restaurants. However, with a rise in immigrants from Asia, Chinese and Indian restaurants were springing up and their relatively affordable and tasty food became so popular that Vesta brought out their first 'foreign convenience' foods, the Vesta Curries and Vesta Chow Mein.

A cheaper alternative was inviting friends to eat at home, and the dinner party boomed from the end of the decade. Pre-dinner drinks were often served with cubes of tinned pineapple and cheddar cheese on sticks, stuck into half a tinfoil covered grapefruit to look like a hedgehog – the height of 60s sophistication! The main course might feature the fashionable 'spaghetti bolognese', and 'Blue Nun', Mateus Rosé or Chianti wine, adding a hint of sophistication to the new 'smart' set's evening.

60s Leisure - Easier

```
G D S V B O L O G N E S E S J
H D U S X S P V R A M I Q Y Q
C I I R Z T A S E T X Q B U F
A N T O H N C P A Z S C A M I
E N N T O A K S S Q E Z E C T
B E A A Y R A I Y Q L H R C N
A R I R M U G R S L T O A U A
H P D E A A E C P S S P F J I
E A N P R T H D O Y A C L N H
D R I O A S O E O E C I A W C
G T E R C E L T N K D D C X O
E Y I U A R I L H N N I O H T
H Y V O S O D A Y O A L L X J
O E E T E R A S X D S H C X L
G F E T H A Y L E S E N I H C
```

PACKAGE HOLIDAY   SANDCASTLES   DONKEYS   BEACH

TOUR OPERATORS   LOCAL FARE   RESTAURANTS   MARACAS

GREASY SPOON   SALTED CRISPS CHINESE   INDIAN

DINNER PARTY   HEDGEHOG   BOLOGNESE   CHIANTI

2nd isle of wight festival of music 1969

Teenage Leisure

The 60's became the era for the teenager, but it started off with the same disciplines as the fifties. At school the teachers commanded respect and gave out punishment when it was not given. Parents could determine when and where their children could be out of house, gave sons and daughters chores to do and families ate together and watched television together.

Scouts and Guides were still very popular and a natural progression from the years as Cubs and Brownies and Outward Bounding or working for the Duke of Edinburgh Awards remained popular for many, but as the decade wore on, the lure of the new found freedom for the young was hard for many to overcome. Coffee bars became the place to meet, drink coffee or chocolate, listen to the latest hits on the juke box and talk with friends. The political climate influenced them, they demonstrated in the streets against the Vietnam War, for civil rights and to 'Ban the Bomb'. They developed the 'hippie' point of view, advocating non-violence and love, and by the end of the decade, "Make Love not War" was the 'flower children's' mantra.

Outdoor music festivals sprang up all over the country and thousands of, usually mud-caked, teenagers gathered to listen to their favourite artists, rock concerts played to packed houses and the young experimented with marijuana and LSD. Psychedelic art was incorporated into films, epitomised by the Beatles' 'Yellow Submarine'.

60s LEISURE - HARDER

```
F  E  S  T  I  V  A  L  S  R  A  W  M  A  N  T  E  I  V  V
X  I  M  X  S  W  S  K  A  D  R  A  W  T  U  O  O  B  N  N
K  B  Q  D  E  P  O  P  U  L  A  R  A  P  V  L  Q  L  Y  X
I  Y  U  C  L  J  V  H  D  E  H  C  T  A  W  J  C  L  K  Y
S  R  D  Q  T  E  L  E  V  I  S  I  O  N  K  M  I  Y  H  Z
S  O  N  S  A  N  D  D  A  U  G  H  T  E  R  S  Z  E  G  X
Z  E  Z  K  E  X  O  B  E  K  U  J  G  B  W  O  M  R  R  H
E  I  D  Q  B  S  E  I  L  I  M  A  F  A  K  O  S  U  U  O
B  T  C  I  V  I  L  R  I  G  H  T  S  E  D  L  F  S  B  Q
P  D  A  L  U  U  T  X  G  P  U  D  S  E  D  L  E  I  N  N
Y  F  E  R  P  G  M  S  P  F  W  J  E  Z  O  U  T  E  I  U
P  S  Y  S  T  U  D  R  E  S  Q  R  V  W  X  N  F  L  D  E
R  R  V  C  T  S  K  N  O  I  F  H  E  X  E  U  P  E  E  R
R  E  K  O  F  R  N  S  A  C  N  R  I  M  D  Z  H  G  F  F
X  H  N  N  S  E  N  O  O  S  P  W  H  P  A  M  H  A  O  M
C  C  D  C  L  S  C  F  M  O  T  S  O  X  P  C  B  N  E  K
J  A  P  E  C  P  F  P  W  E  I  U  T  R  W  I  Y  E  K  I
X  E  O  R  K  E  R  E  P  N  D  U  O  H  B  V  E  E  U  R
U  T  I  T  E  C  R  O  U  D  A  I  C  C  D  B  Z  T  D  G
P  D  Z  S  F  T  W  P  S  I  C  U  U  H  S  U  N  C  D  G
```

TEENAGE LEISURE	**TEACHERS**	**RESPECT**	**PUNISHMENT**
SONS AND DAUGHTERS	**FAMILIES**	**WATCHED**	**TELEVISION**
SCOUTS AND GUIDES	**POPULAR**	**BROWNIES**	**OUTWARD**
DUKE OF EDINBURGH	**FREEDOM**	**JUKE BOX**	**COFFEE**
VIETNAM WAR	**DEMONSTRATE**	**CIVIL RIGHTS**	**HIPPIE**
FLOWER POWER	**FESTIVALS**	**CONCERTS**	**BEATLES**

1960 **Poor Me by Adam Faith**, a teen idol, reached number 1 and stayed there for two weeks whilst his previous number 1 hit, **What Do You Want** was still in the top ten. The Everly Brothers, the American rock duo, had their fifth number 1 with **Cathy's Clown**. Their first was Bye Bye Love in 1957. A surprise number 1 for four weeks was by Lonnie Donnegan, the skiffle singer, with **My Old Man's a Dustman.**

1961 **Wooden Heart** sung by Elvis Presley stayed at number 1 for six weeks and became the best-selling UK single of the year. Johnny Leyton had a three-week number 1 with **Johnny Remember Me** in August and it returned to the number 1 spot again at the end of September. Teenage singer and actress Helen Shapiro, had her second number one, **Walkin' Back to Happiness**, whilst still only fifteen.

1962 The top selling single of the year was by the Australian singer, Frank Ifield. **I Remember You** was sung in a yodelling, country-music style.
Acker Bilk's **Stranger on the Shore** becomes the first British recording to reach the number 1 spot on the US Billboard Hot 100.
The Rolling Stones make their debut at London's Marquee Club, opening for Long John Baldry.

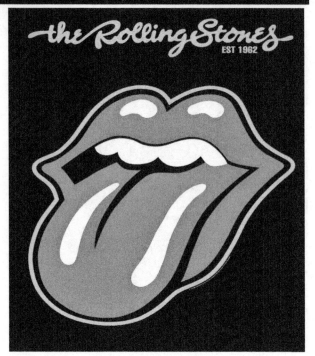

1962: The Rolling Stones make their debut at London's Marquee Club playing the rock n' roll of Chuck Berry and Bo Diddley.

1963 The Beatles have three number 1's in the UK charts in their first year. **From Me to You, She Loves You** and **I Want to Hold Your Hand.** Their debut album, **Please Please Me**, reaches the top of the album charts.
Produced by Phil Spector, The Crystals have a hit with **And Then He Kissed Me**
How Do You Do What You Do to Me, the debut single by Liverpudlian band Gerry and the Pacemakers, stays at number 1 for three weeks in April.

1964 The Hollies, the Merseybeat group founded by school friends Allan Clarke and Graham Nash, reach number 2 in the UK charts with **Just One Look**, a cover of the song by Doris Troy in the US.
Originally written by Burt Bacharach for Dionne Warwick, **Anyone Who Had a** Heart, sung by Cilla Black, became a UK number 1 for three weeks and was also the fourth best-selling single of 1964 in the UK, with sales of around 950,000 copies.

"The Fab Four", John Lennon, Paul McCartney, George Harrison and Ringo Star were the ultimate pop phenomenon of the '60s.

```
E  W  S  E  L  T  A  E  B  E  H  T  T  N  G
B  I  L  L  B  O  A  R  D  H  F  F  A  Z  S
I  H  W  U  C  H  U  C  K  B  E  R  R  Y  N
A  T  S  S  T  O  N  E  S  P  S  G  H  I  L
M  I  R  R  N  K  M  K  C  H  K  S  Y  Q  O
C  A  E  A  C  K  E  R  B  I  L  K  L  A  N
I  F  K  D  I  O  N  N  E  L  C  I  R  E  G
L  M  A  S  E  I  X  Z  X  S  R  F  E  I  J
L  A  M  X  J  F  G  C  A  P  Y  M  V  K  O
A  D  E  L  V  I  S  P  R  E  S  L  E  Y  H
B  A  C  N  E  R  X  H  K  C  T  R  Q  F  N
L  M  A  R  Q  U  E  E  Y  T  A  F  S  R  U
A  A  P  S  O  J  H  G  O  O  L  C  R  Z  V
C  O  Z  F  J  O  Y  X  Z  R  S  T  K  S  O
K  Z  C  N  A  I  L  D  U  P  R  E  V  I  L
```

ADAM FAITH	**EVERLY**	**ELVIS PRESLEY**	**ACKER BILK**
MARQUEE	**STONES**	**BILLBOARD**	**LONG JOHN**
CHUCK BERRY	**THE BEATLES**	**PHIL SPECTOR**	**CRYSTALS**
PACEMAKERS	**LIVERPUDLIAN**	**CILLA BLACK**	**DIONNE**

1965 Unchained Melody by The Righteous Brothers, with a solo by Bobby Hatfield becomes a jukebox standard. **Its Not Unusual** sung by Tom Jones becomes an international hit after being promoted by the offshore, pirate radio station, Radio Caroline. **Get Off of My Cloud** by The Rolling Stones was written by Mick Jagger and Keith Richards as a single to follow their previous hit of the year, **(I Can't Get No) Satisfaction**.

1966 Nancy Sinatra with **These Boots Are Made for Walkin'** reaches number 1.
Good Vibrations sung by The Beach Boys, becomes an immediate hit both sides of the Atlantic.
Ike and Tina Turner released **River Deep, Mountain High** and their popularity soars in the UK after a tour with The Rolling Stones.

1967 Waterloo Sunset by The Kinks, written by Ray Davies, reached number 2 in the British charts and was a top 10 hit in Australia, New Zealand and most of Europe. In North America, it failed to chart.
A Whiter Shade of Pale the debut single by Procul Harem stays at number 1 for eight weeks.
Sandie Shaw wins the Eurovision Song Contest with **Puppet on a String**.

1968 Dusty Springfield's **Son of a Preacher Man** was her last top thirty hit until her collaboration with The Pet Shop Boys in 1987. In 1994, **Preacher Man** was included in Tarantino's film 'Pulp Fiction'.
Manfred Mann has a resounding success with **Mighty Quinn**, their third UK number 1 and third hit singing a song written by Bob Dylan.
The comedy group The Scaffold's record, **Lily the Pink** released in November became number 1 for the four weeks over the Christmas holidays.

1969 **Where Do You Go To (My Lovely)?** by the British singer-songwriter Peter Sarstedt stayed at number 1 for four weeks.
I Heard It Through the Grapevine was written in 1966 and recorded by Gladys Knight and the Pips. However, it was the version by Marvin Gaye that took the number 1 spot in the UK for three weeks and became the biggest hit single on the Motown label.
Je t'aime... moi non plus was written in 1967 for Brigitte Bardot but Serge Gainsbourg and Jane Birkin recorded the best known version and the duet reached number 1 in the UK. It was banned in several countries due to its overtly sexual content.

MUSIC IN THE 60s - HARDER

```
S E X K L I E L Y K T O V D C E B C B U
J D O B S X R F A S M A R V I N G A Y E
B U T O R X I C F Y Y V T N L M L Q J H
V S H T E W Q V P E Q O A B O S L V Y T
Y T E D H G A X I W U L B T E P V G F M
L Y P S T R G T S R Y R O H R E N R U T
P S I D O A X O E D K W O G C U M Q P E
R P P R R P K L N R N V W V C A L R W T
E R S A B E X M O I L I T I I I E B S N
A I E H S V J N J B X O T E C S L B M A
C N I C U I C U M S D N O L S Q I F I N
H G D I O N A N O M A T L S D R J O M C
E F N R E E R X T L Y U H C U L J A N Y
R I A H T N O Z T F N A C E Y N N P J S
D E S T H Q L A Y D O L E M K F S A Q I
J L Z I G T I Y J Z F W U K R I G E D N
K D Z E I L N A R I T A V E S G N Y T A
C E U K R J E S Q N N B D M E X S K K T
Q P S T O N E S P J O R R R H D H W S R
N O I T C A F S I T A S E J A S D I B A
```

RIGHTEOUS BROTHERS	**MELODY**	**TOM JONES**	**STONES**
KEITH RICHARDS	**SATISFACTION**	**CAROLINE**	**JAGGER**
NANCY SINATRA	**BEACH BOYS**	**ATLANTIC**	**TURNER**
WATERLOO SUNSET	**THE KINKS**	**EUROVISION**	**SANDIE**
DUSTY SPRINGFIELD	**PREACHER**	**MANFRED**	**DYLAN**
MARVIN GAYE	**GRAPEVINE**	**MOTOWN**	**THE PIPS**

The London Smog

Britain still experienced "pea-soupers" in the 60's and in December 1962, London suffered under a choking blanket of smog. After three days, the noxious layer spread all over the country.

Smog is a concentration of smoke particles and other substances such as sulphur dioxide, combined with fog in conditions of low temperature, high pressure and lack of wind. Visibility was reduced such that a light could only be seen at 50ft and in spite of people covering their faces with scarves, surgical masks or handkerchiefs, the overwhelming smell of sulphur and coal smoke left an unpleasant metallic taste in the mouth and irritated eyes and noses. Bronchitis increased significantly and it is estimated that, in Greater London alone, there were 700 deaths in total.

In 1962, the Duke of Edinburgh was in New York for the inaugural dinner of the US branch of the World Wildlife Fund, first set up in Zurich in 1961, and warned his audience that our descendants could be forced to live in a world where the only living creature would be man himself -"*always assuming,*" he said, "*that we don't destroy ourselves as well in the meantime.*"

In his speech, the Duke described poachers who were threatening extermination of many big game animals in Africa as "killers for profit ... the get-rich-at-any-price mob." African poachers, he said, were killing off the rhinoceros to get its horn for export to China, "*where, for some incomprehensible reason, they seem to think it acts as an aphrodisiac.*" The Duke also criticised the status seekers – people "like the eagle chasers". The bald eagle in North America was being chased and killed by people in light aeroplanes who seem to think it smart to own its feathers and claws.

"*What is needed, above all now,*" he said, "*are people all over the world who understand the problem and really care about it. People who have the courage to see that the conservation laws are obeyed.*"

Duke of Edinburgh Launches World Wildlife Fund

```
E K O M S P O A C H E R S D A
K E T O Q L B G N M O C Y H N
C O D Y E O J A B G Y D T I O
U L M D F W D O A L B K I P I
Z M R X I T L I L Z R S L S T
G R E R L E O R D A O O I R A
X H D P D M N U E E N R B E V
Z G U E L P D H A R C E I H R
K R C A I E O P G O H C S T E
U U E S W R N L L P I O I A S
R B D O D A S U E L T N V E N
S N N U L T M S V A I I G F O
H I M P R U O M H N S H P Q C
J D E E O R G U P E L R B O E
P E Y R W E A S N S X O A Q F
```

LONDON SMOG	**PEA SOUPER**	**SMOKE**	**SULPHUR**
LOW TEMPERATURE	**VISIBILITY**	**REDUCED**	**BRONCHITIS**
WORLD WILDLIFE	**EDINBURGH**	**POACHERS**	**RHINOCEROS**
BALD EAGLE	**AEROPLANES**	**FEATHERS**	**CONSERVATION**

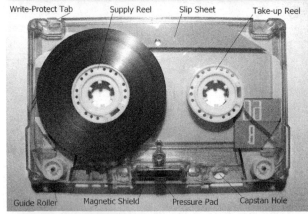

Write-Protect Tab   Supply Reel   Slip Sheet   Take-up Reel

Guide Roller   Magnetic Shield   Pressure Pad   Capstan Hole

THE CASSETTE TAPE

The cassette tape was first developed by Philips in Belgium in 1962. These two small spools inside its plastic case, which wind magnetic-coated film on which the audio content is stored and pass it from one side to the other, meant music could now be recorded and shared by everyone.

Up until now, music was typically recorded on vinyl which needed a record player, or on reel-to-reel recorders which were comparatively expensive and difficult to use and neither of which were portable. The cassette player allowed individuals to record their favourite songs easily and also take their music with them "on-the-go". Music lovers soon learned how to create their own mixed tapes, for themselves or to share with friends.

More than 3 billion tapes were sold between 1962 and 1988.

THE ABERFAN DISASTER

On 21 October 1966, the worst mining-related disaster in British history took place in Aberfan, in South Wales. Coal was mined there for domestic heating and the waste was dumped at the top of the valley on land of no economic value. But crucially, it was tipped on highly porous sandstone which overlaid at least one natural spring.

During October 1966 heavy rainfall led to a build-up of water within this tip and caused it to collapse. With a deafening roar, 107 cu m of black slurry turned into an avalanche. The deluge leapt over the old railway embankment into the village where destroyed 18 houses and Pant Glas Junior School together with part of the neighbouring County Secondary School.

In total, 144 lives were lost, 116 of them children, 109 of these were aged between seven and ten and died in their classrooms on the last day before half term. Of the 28 adults who died, five were primary school teachers.

The official inquiry placed the blame entirely on the National Coal Board.

SCIENCE & NATURE - HARDER

```
Q R E T S A S I D N A F R E B A L S S P
E S C I E N C E A N D N A T U R E P Q G
E S A C C I T S A L P F C B R L D W C D
B Y M U I G L E B W S O M E F E R L D O
L M A G N E T I C D L Q C J S E A H E T
C F V R B W K U F L J O R F O R O W R S
N B O K W X B N A P R Y D J Q O B D A P
Y G J F N Y C P A D Q A P E P T L O H I
B K U Y H B S O P T P W J K L L A M S L
Q B N S F E P L A A U E H R C E O E S I
P L I H P B A O W L D R J Q L E C S D H
E A O W A Y T V R N M C A W A R T T N P
T M R W E A H S Y T L I D L S Y L I E K
T E S R U B N G D R A O N Z S A F C I F
E R C V G Y A N D M A B L E R P A H R S
S M H J E B H E W R Y I L S O A R K F E
S F O G O G L I Z S L K N E O C U I O C
A F O B S U C I W U E I L P M R F E N U
C C L E G S E L A W H T U O S F R A S G
T R B E E P R R E C O R D E D T P P L G
```

SCIENCE AND NATURE CASSETTE PHILIPS BELGIUM
PLASTIC CASE MAGNETIC RECORDED SHARED
RECORD PLAYER REEL TO REEL PORTABLE FRIENDS
ABERFAN DISASTER SOUTH WALES COAL MINE DOMESTIC
NATURAL SPRING HEAVY RAIN COLLAPSE DELUGE
JUNIOR SCHOOL CLASSROOMS COAL BOARD BLAME

1960 - 1969

1960 In tennis, Rod Laver wins his first grand slam title as a 21-year-old taking the **Australian Open.**
Jack Brabham wins the **F1 driver's championship** for the second straight time.

1961 **Five Nations Championship** (now 6 Nations) rugby series is won by France.
Tottenham Hotspur beat Leicester City 2-0 in the **FA Cup Final**.

1962 Sonny Liston knocks out Floyd Pattison after two minutes into the first round of the "Boxing World Title" fight in Chicago.

1963 Mill House, at 18 hands, known as 'The Big Horse', wins the **Cheltenham Gold Cup.**

1964 The **Tour de France i**s won by Jacques Anquetil of France, the first cyclist to win the Tour five times. 1957 and 1961-64.

1965 At the **Masters** in Atlanta, Jack Nicklaus shoots a record 17 under par to win the tournament.
In the **FA Cup Final** at Wembley, Liverpool beats Leeds United 2-1.

1966 England defeat Germany to win the **FIFA World Cup**

1967 Defending champion Billie Jean King defeats Ann Haydon-Jones in the **Wimbledon Women's Singles Championship**.
The New York Yacht Club retains the **America's Cup** when 'Intrepid' beat the Australian challenger 'Dame Pattie', 4 races to 1.

1968 English International cricketer Basil D'Oliveira, of 'Cape Coloured' background, is excluded from the **MCC South African tour** side, leading to turmoil in the world of cricket.

1969 **The Grand National i**s won by 12-year-old Highland Wedding by 12 lengths.

1966 FIFA World Cup

On July 30th, England and West Germany lined up at Wembley to determine the winner of the 'Jules Rimet Trophy', the prize for winning the World Cup. England won 4-2 after extra time and the match is remembered for Geoff Hurst's hat-trick and the controversial third goal awarded to England by the referee and linesman.

In addition to an attendance of 96,924 at the stadium, the British television audience peaked at 32.3 million viewers, making it the UK's most-watched television event ever.

It was the first occasion that England had hosted, or won, the World Cup and was to remain their only major tournament win. It was also the nation's last final at a major international football tournament for 55 years, until 2021 when England reached the Euro Final but lost to Italy after a penalty shootout.

60s Sport - Easier

```
V O N E M X H S G H O J H L T
M F S X A B T P R I F E R F G
A Z T U H L P L A H D A C Z E
H Y O P N A U P N Z P N T S O
N F U U E N C Q D E R K W N F
E T R C T I D H N X B I I O F
T E D S L F L A A T D N M I H
T M E A E P R T T R V G B T I
O I F C H U O T I A I N L A R
T R R I C C W R O T L D E N S
R S A R Q A Z I N I Z H D E T
V E N E P F V C A M X L O V K
Z L C M Z N O K L E A Y N I I
W U E A L I N E S M A N H F U
H J S U A L K C I N K C A J K
```

FIVE NATIONS   **TOTTENHAM**   **FA CUP FINAL**   **CHELTENHAM**

TOUR DE FRANCE   **JACK NICKLAUS**   **WORLD CUP**   **WIMBLEDON**

GRAND NATIONAL   **AMERICAS CUP**   **JEAN KING**   **JULES RIMET**

EXTRA TIME   **GEOFF HIRST**   **LINESMAN**   **HAT TRICK**

1964 OLYMPIC GAMES

In 1964, the first Olympic Games to be held in Asia, took place in Japan during October to avoid the city's midsummer heat and humidity and the September typhoon season. It marked many milestones in the history of the modern Games; a cinder running track was used for the last time in the athletics events, whilst a fibreglass pole was used for the first time in the pole-vaulting competition. These Games were also the last occasion that hand timing by stopwatch was used for official timing.

25 world records were broken and 52 of a possible 61 Olympic records were also broken. Ethiopian runner Abebe Bikila won his second consecutive Olympic marathon. Bob Hayes won the men's 100 metres and then anchored the US 400 metre relay team to a world record victory. Peter Snell, the New Zealand middle-distance runner, won both the 800 and 1500 metres, the only man to have done so in the same Olympics since 1920. Ann Packer of Britain made a record-breaking debut winning gold in the 800 metres and silver in the 400 metres.

Peter Snell, winning the 1500 metres.

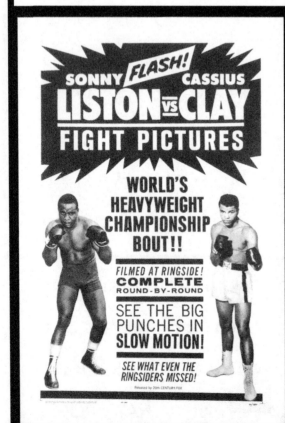

CASSIUS CLAY HEAVYWEIGHT CHAMPION OF THE WORLD

In 1964, Cassius Clay, later this year to be known as Muhammad Ali, fought and gained Sonny Liston's title of Heavyweight Champion of the World. The big fight took place in Miami Beach in February.

Liston was an intimidating fighter and Clay was the 7-1 under-dog, but still he engaged in taunting his opponent during the build-up to the fight, dubbing him *"the big ugly bear"*, stating *"Liston even smells like a bear"* and claiming, *"After I beat him, I'm going to donate him to the zoo!"*
The result of the fight was a major upset as Clay's speed and mobility kept him out of trouble and in the third round hit Liston with a combination that opened a cut under his left eye and eventually, Liston could not come out for the seventh round.
A triumphant Clay rushed to the edge of the ring and, pointing to the ringside press, shouted: *"Eat your words!"* adding the words he was to live up to for the rest of his life, *"I am the greatest!"*

60s Sport - Harder

```
P A N A I P O I H T E I X Y T W H I P L
N O H T A R A M M R F H Z S H D E L M Y
H L L E N S R E T E P J E C H U A X I A
U Q U P G L Q S C B S T A W P I V Q N L
R Y L H U V C U X M A T N P C Q Y N O C
W D A M M A H U M E L C T I A S W O I S
Q H X R O A F T R T X L F E G N E T T U
S E U N E O W G P P K F H L N O I S I I
L E K M N B E D Q E O P C O I S G I T S
M U M B I H O W B S O C T P A H L E S
W M I A T D G T U O T G A S N E T S P A
K I B O G H I Y C B C Q W S U S C C M C
C A M O O C S T I O D C P A A N N I O R
L M G O I X I R Y Z H S O L T O H T C E
R I S O L O Y P N A F F T G B O E E J D
N B Q I U O C D M Z D M S E R H T L K N
K E F U R Z R P A Y A I M R I P O H Z I
S A N Q W J I B P H L B N B X Y R T B C
C C D E R O H C N A R O R I B T Y A S Y
C H Y T N S T Q E Y G K B F I T B B F T
```

OLYMPIC GAMES
TYPHOON SEASON
FIBREGLASS POLE
ETHIOPIAN
CASSIUS CLAY
MIAMI BEACH

OCTOBER
SEPTEMBER
STOPWATCH
MARATHON
HEAVYWEIGHT
TAUNTING

JAPAN
CINDER
OFFICIAL
ANCHORED
CHAMPION
LISTON

HUMIDITY
ATHLETICS
COMPETITION
PETER SNELL
MUHAMMAD
THE GREATEST

Trolleybuses were taken out of service in London in May having served since 1931.

How luxurious can an Austin Seven get?

The revolutionary Mini was the fastest selling small car in Britain in the 60s. Despite the promise of the adverts early models were slow and unreliable and although promoted as a luxury family car, it was uncomfortable and cramped.

THE VICKERS VC10

The 60's produced Britain's biggest airliner to date, the four jet Vickers VC10. With a towering tailplane, high as a four-storey house, the airliner weighed 150 tons fully loaded and was 158ft long. In service with BOAC and other airlines from the end of 1963 until 1981, the plane could carry 150 passengers at flew at 600mph over distances exceeding 4,000 miles. From 1965 they were also used as strategic air transports for the RAF.

CARS OF THE DECADE

The importance of personal transport increased dramatically during the Sixties and three of the images inextricably linked with the decade are the three-wheeler 'bubble car', the sleek, sexy, elongated E-type Jaguar and VW Camper Van.

```
G T X F B F R E D A C E D T B
U L G K I Q U O T P R B Z U O
T T L L G E N G F W A C H N R
R R N I G P R M C G U N U C W
O O E A E A E E R H G K N O Z
P L V T S S L R A A A V A M S
S L E G T S I A M M J N V F T
N E S N A E A C P Z N O R O R
A Y N I I N B E E T T D E R A
R B I R R G L L D D S N P T T
T U T E L E E B W F E O M A E
D S S W I R W B L V T L A B G
Z E U O N S E U J C S C C L I
O S A T E B K B V T A C W E C
D M U S R G Q Y U O F G V L L
```

TRANSPORT	TROLLEY BUSES	LONDON	FASTEST
AUSTIN SEVEN	UNCOMFORTABLE	UNRELIABLE	CRAMPED
BIGGEST AIRLINER	TOWERING TAIL	PASSENGERS	STRATEGIC
VW CAMPER VAN	BUBBLE CAR	JAGUAR	DECADE

MODS AND ROCKERS
SCOOTERS v MOTOR BIKES

Mods and Rockers were two rival British youth sub-cultures of the 1960's with a tendency to riot on Brighton beach.

They had very different outlooks: The Mods thought of themselves as sophisticated, stylish and in touch with the times. The motor cycling centred Rockers thought the Mods effeminate snobs!

They had very different appearances: Mods centred on fashion and wore suits or other clean-cut outfits. The Rockers wore black leather jackets and motorcycle boots or sometimes, 'brothel creeper' shoes.

They had very different tastes in music. The Mods favoured Soul and African American R&B. The Rockers went for Rock 'n Roll.

So not surprisingly, they had very different tastes in transport.

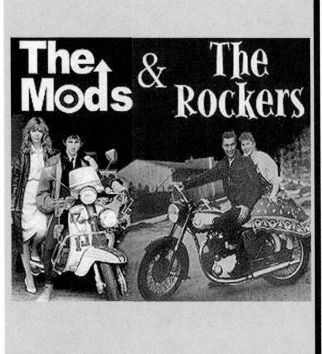

THE HOVERCRAFT

The great British invention of the decade was the Hovercraft. It was developed by Briton, Sir Christopher Cockerell. Saunders Roe, the flying boat firm at Cowes on the Isle of Wight built the prototype SR.N1, 20ft craft which first took to the seas in July 1959, crossing the English Channel from Calais to Dover in two hours with the inventor onboard. In 1961 hovercraft skirts were introduced to the design which provided far greater performance abilities and sea keeping.

The Hovercraft was a revolution in sea travel and the 1960's saw a fleet of craft crossing from the south coast to the Isle of Wight. They are now used throughout the world as specialised transports in disaster relief, coastguard, military and survey applications, as well as for sport or passenger service.

60s Transport - Harder

```
R E P E E R C D X H D S E A T R A V E L
Q U N O S R E H T A E L G N I S S O R C
G V Z Z C E U R I X A Y J L J O P J V P
A G N M P D E T A C I T S I H P O S J R
O V O H Y S S Q X B R I T I S H Y Q X O
S I I C C T T N I J I Q H N G M Q D V T
U L T A I A H I O R C U W E W S O N C O
B B N E S F L E F B N Z O R Z C L X H T
C U E B L P G A H T S A Z M C O C P R Y
U N V N E E H M I O U U D O U O O K I P
L U N O O N K R I S V O E S G T G S S E
T G I T F G N Z Z L T E T Y C E D N T Q
U N X H W L I J U C I O R U B R K S O A
R S C G I I Y A I T I T D C C S K R P O
E C V I G S O I J B W S A O R N Q W H I
L Y R R H H B F N K Z G U R V A A X E A
M W L B T W P W P G N F V M Y E F E R C
H S R E K C O R D N A S D O M F R T L L
U S E K I B R O T O M C H A N N E L A C
V C N T M O W C A J B A T T K Q X Y R K
```

MODS AND ROCKERS
BRIGHTON BEACH
CLEAN CUT OUTFITS
THE HOVERCRAFT
ISLE OF WIGHT
CALAIS TO DOVER

SCOOTERS
SUB CULTURE
CREEPER
INVENTION
PROTOTYPE
SEA TRAVEL

MOTOR BIKES
SOPHISTICATED
LEATHERS
CHRISTOPHER
ENGLISH
CROSSING

BRITISH
SNOBS
MUSIC
FLYING
CHANNEL
MILITARY

1947: Britain was struck this year by 'the perfect storm'. Record snowfall followed by a sudden thaw which culminated in heavy rain produced what is widely considered to be Britain's worst flood. Over 100,000 homes were directly affected and over 750,000 hectares of farmland submerged. The damages at the time totalled around £12 million, £300 million in today's terms.

1952: In August, the tiny village of Lynmouth, north Devon, suffered the worst river flood in English history. On the 15th, just over 9in (230mm) of rain fell over north Devon and west Somerset. The East and West Lyn rivers flooded and tons of water, soil, boulders and vegetation descended over Exmoor to meet at sea level in Lynmouth. The village was destroyed. The West Lyn rose 60 ft (18.25 m) above the normal level at its highest point and 34 people lost their lives.

1963: Britain had the coldest winter in living memory, lasting for three long months from Dec 1962. The 6th March 1963 was the first morning of the year without frost anywhere in Britain.
It was so cold that rivers, lakes and even the sea froze over. On 25 February a record low of -22c in Braemar was recorded and 95,000 miles of road were snowbound.

1953: The great North Sea flood of January caused catastrophic damage and loss of life in Scotland, England, Belgium and The Netherlands and was Britain's worst peacetime disaster on record claiming the lives of 307 people. There were no severe flood warnings in place and the combination of gale-force winds, low pressure and high tides brought havoc to over 1,000 miles of coastline and 32,000 people were displaced because of flooding.

1987: The Hurricane that wasn't supposed to be! Weatherman Michael Fish, like other forecasters, didn't see it coming. Eighteen people died and over 15 million trees were lost when in October, the hurricane-force winds blasted through south-east England. Meteorological research revealed a completely new weather phenomenon called the 'sting jet', a 100mph wind, the first to be documented in Britain.

WEATHER - EASIER

```
M F I Y A L L A F W O N S F E
M D N A L T O C S J X R Y Q H
W H B P K A L Y N M O U T H R
S E E N C O V Z G N F M W S W
E N N O U P T T F A O L E R F
D A I R W G G F W E R G A G E
I C L T S D N A L R E H T E N
T I T H X K I A P E C F H M G
H R S S S H D X X B A M E U L
G R A E R Q O V U O S J R I A
I U O A M G O V R T T H X G N
H H C Z X P L L Y C E L Z L D
H Z M H J I F X O O R Q C E B
Q P E R F E C T S T O R M B Z
J U V U N I A T I R B Y X D U
```

PERFECT STORM   SNOWFALL   BRITAIN   LYNMOUTH

NORTH SEA   SCOTLAND   ENGLAND   BELGIUM

NETHERLANDS   HIGH TIDES   FLOODING   COASTLINE

HURRICANE   FORECASTER   OCTOBER   WEATHER

2003: In August a new UK record was set for the 'Hottest Day in History' when temperatures reached 38.5c (101.3f) in Faversham, Kent. By the end of the summer, the heat had claimed the lives of over 2,000 people in Britain, mostly through heat stroke or dehydration.

An almost empty reservoir

2004: A flash flood submerged the Cornish village of Boscastle during the busy holiday period when over 60 mm of rain (typically a month's rainfall) fell in two hours. The ground was already saturated due to two weeks of above average rainfall and the Jordan and Valency rivers burst their banks causing about two billion litres of water to rush down the valley straight into Boscastle. This led to the flash flood which caused total devastation to the area, but miraculously, no loss of life.

1976: Britain had its hottest three months in living memory and it should have been the perfect summer, but with the continued sunshine came the worst drought in 150 years. Rivers dried up, soil began to crack and water supplies were on the verge of running out in Britain's most dramatic heatwave of the 20th Century. The drought was so rare, Britain appointed its first ever minister for drought, Denis Howell. He was nicknamed the minister for rain as the day after they installed him the heavens opened for the next two months!

2000: Following a wet spring and early summer, the autumn was the wettest on record for over 270 years. Repeated heavy rainfall in October and November caused significant and extensive flooding, inundated 10,000 homes and businesses. Train services cancelled, major motorways closed, and power supplies disrupted.

2007: Summer 2007 was the wettest on record with 414.1mm of rain falling across England and Wales in May, June and July - more than at any time since records began in 1766.
Although the rain was exceptionally heavy, climatologists say it was not the result of global warming. A report by the Centre for Ecology and Hydrology concluded the rain was a freak event, not part of any historical trend.

WEATHER - HARDER

```
Q Q R M P Q A L E C O L O G Y W A L E S
Y E W T Q U R E N I H S N U S Z L S Q M
A O I G L O B A L L D F X T H E B H F O
I B R E T S I N I M S Q L D W V T I A T
M E C A N C E L L E D T C O S A D D Z O
M G N I D O O L F A G P H Z E W E M B R
I N U N D A T E D F C H V B I T H K C W
Q P L W J J Q P V M R Q S X L A Y D P A
X N D W T S E T T E W V F R P E D I Y Y
T O Y V X N G A I S D A I T P H R S O S
H O T T E S T D A Y V O T D U V A R O J
Q D T A B L G P X E V T R P S F T U P G
Y C F P S V P O R R K O W N R J I P D R
R E C O R D S S E U U W P P E I O T B R
F L Y F N D H S T G M B H P W Y N E T R
U B A B O A E K H G J R N F O M D D F E
S V D W M R J T W K I B V U P R R X T M
H P C A P E V I S N E T X E Z E U Q R M
I G C P G N I M R A W R F T V S Z A Z U
Y E I E L S T S I G O L O T A M I L C S
```

HOTTEST DAY	**FAVERSHAM**	**SUMMER**	**DEHYDRATION**
HEATWAVE	**DROUGHT**	**SUNSHINE**	**RESERVOIR**
MINISTER	**HOWELL**	**EXTENSIVE**	**FLOODING**
INUNDATED	**CANCELLED**	**MOTORWAYS**	**DISRUPTED**
POWER SUPPLIES	**WETTEST**	**WALES**	**RECORDS**
CLIMATOLOGISTS	**GLOBAL**	**WARMING**	**ECOLOGY**

SOLUTIONS

PAGE 5

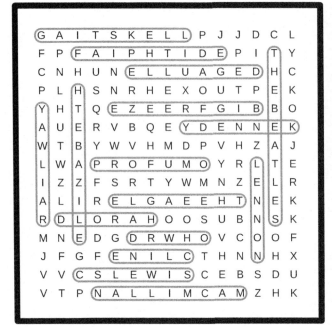

PAGE 7

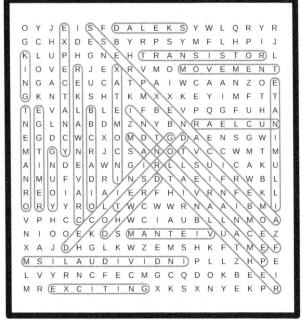

PAGE 9

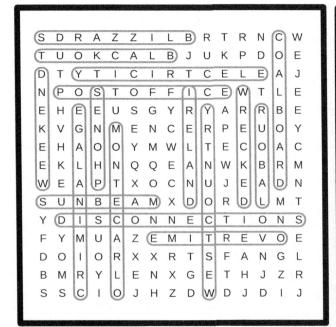

PAGE 11

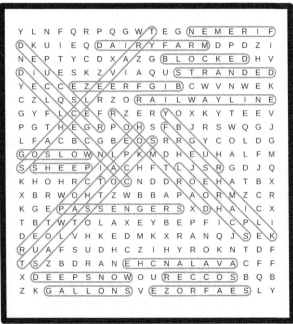

SOLUTIONS

PAGE 13

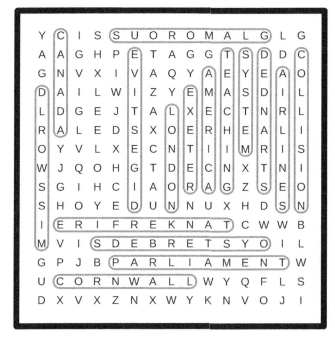

PAGE 15

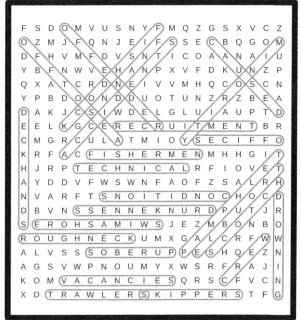

PAGE 17

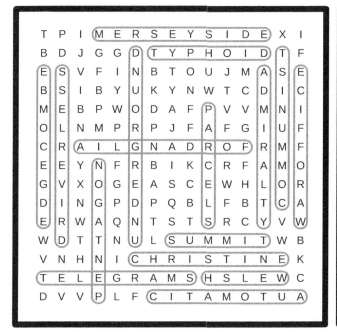

PAGE 19

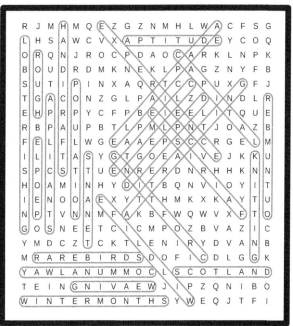

SOLUTIONS

PAGE 21

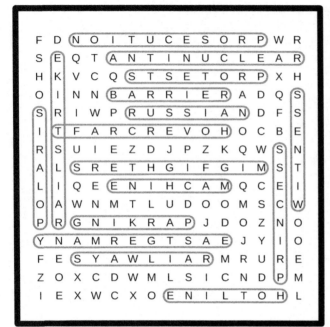

PAGE 23

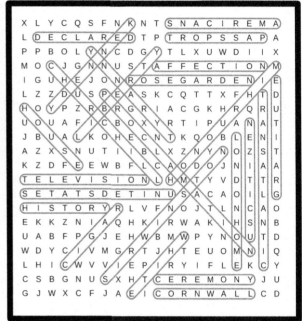

PAGE 25

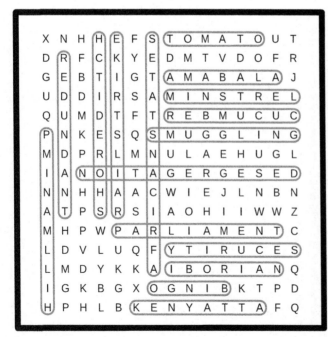

PAGE 27

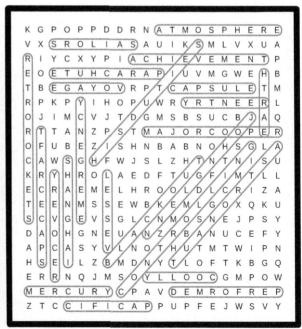

SOLUTIONS

Page 29

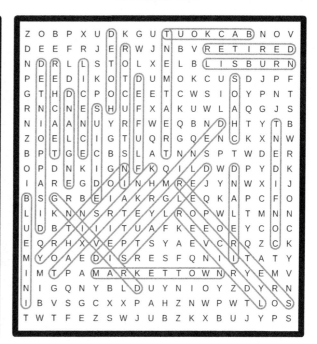

PAGE 31

PAGE 33

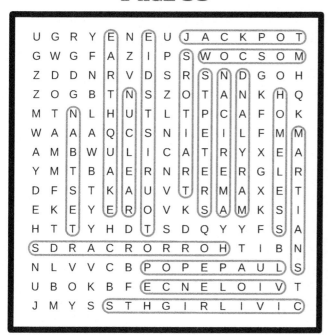

PAGE 35

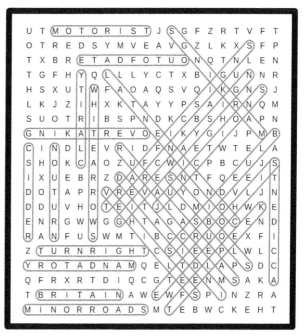

SOLUTIONS

PAGE 37

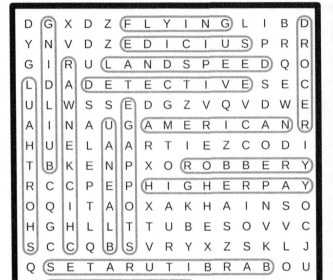

PAGE 39

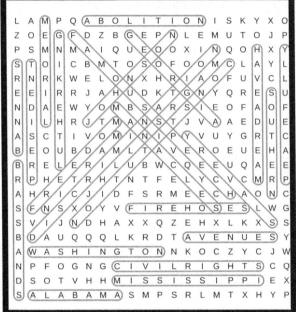

PAGE 41

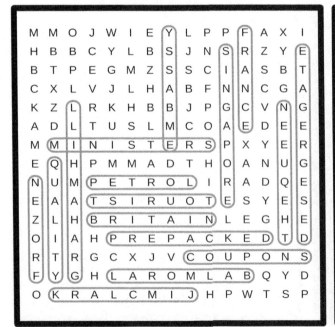

PAGE 43

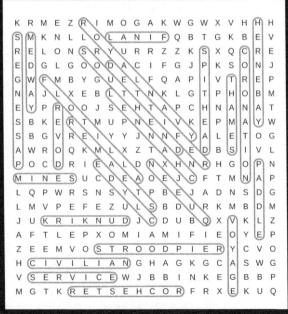

SOLUTIONS

PAGE 45

PAGE 47

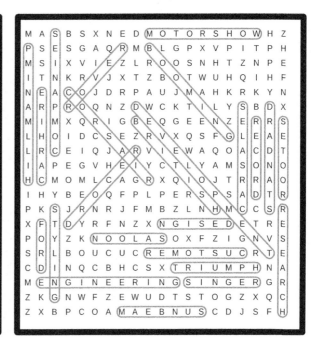

PAGE 49

PAGE 51

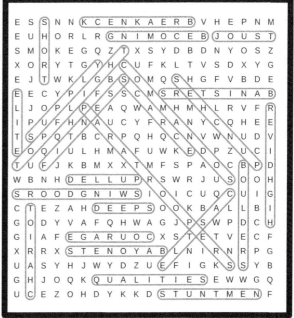

SOLUTIONS

PAGE 53

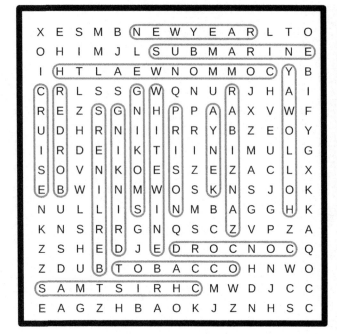

PAGE 55

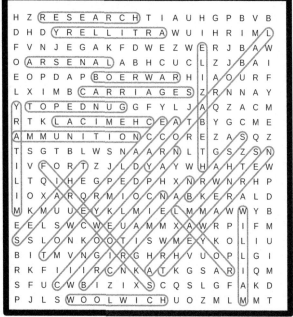

PAGE 57

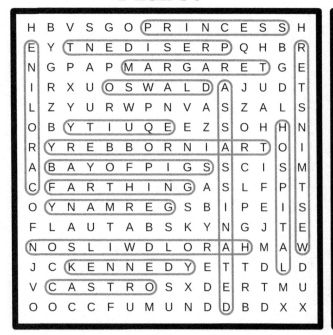

PAGE 59

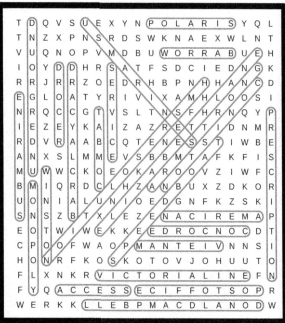

SOLUTIONS

PAGE 61

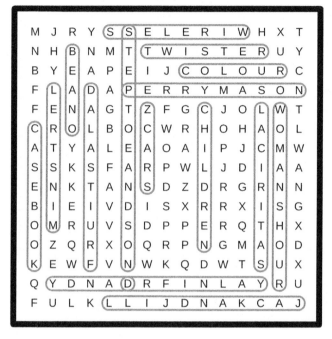

PAGE 63

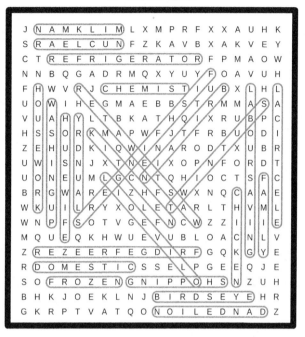

PAGE 65

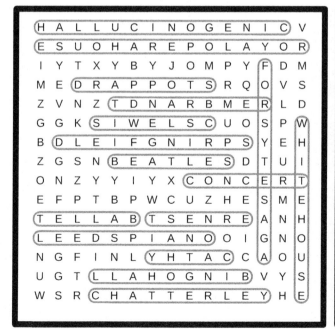

PAGE 67

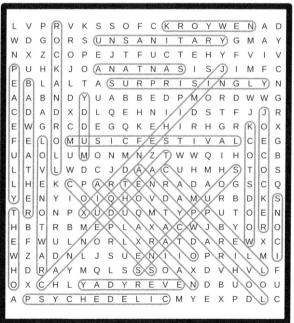

SOLUTIONS

PAGE 69

PAGE 71

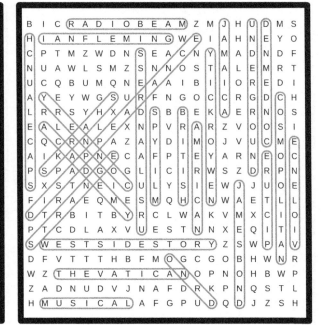

PAGE 73

PAGE 75

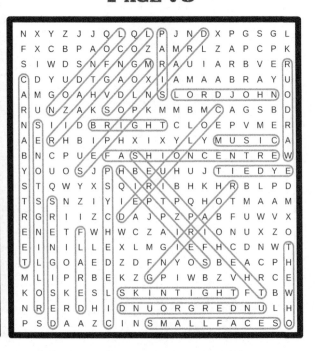

SOLUTIONS

PAGE 77

PAGE 79

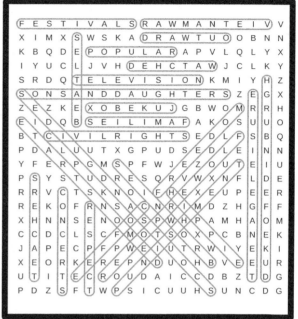

PAGE 81

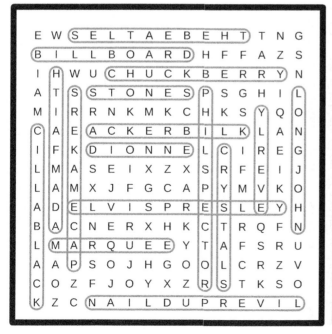

PAGE 83

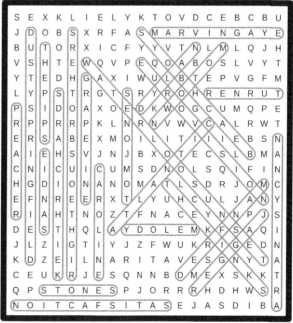

SOLUTIONS

PAGE 85

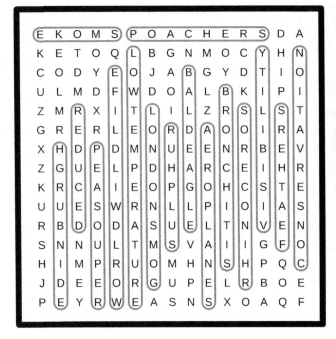

PAGE 87

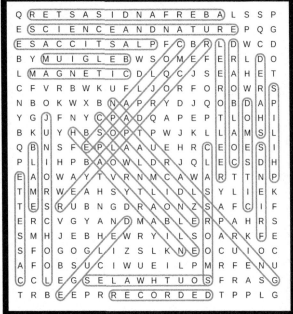

PAGE 89

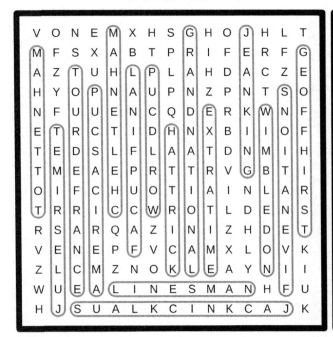

PAGE 91

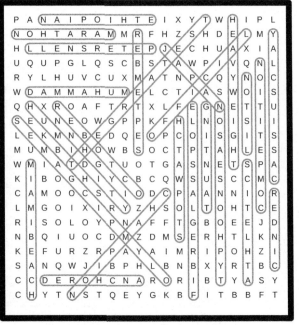

SOLUTIONS

PAGE 93

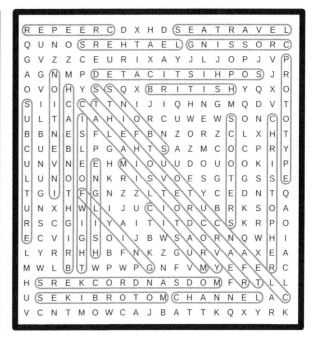

PAGE 95

```
G T X F B F R E D A C E D T B
U L G K I Q U O T P R B Z U O
T T L L G E N G F W A C H N R
R R N I A G P R M C G U N U W
O E E A T G E E R H G K O Z Z
P L V T S S L R A A V A M O S
S E G N T S I A M M J N V F T
N E N A E A C P Z O N O E O R
A Y I N I N B E E T T D N P A
R B R R G L L D D S E N O T T
T U I E L I R W B L V L O T E
D S E W N S E U J C S C A B G
Z U N S E B K B V T A C L E I
O A T E B K B V T A C W E L L
D M U S R G Q Y U O F G V L L
```

PAGE 97

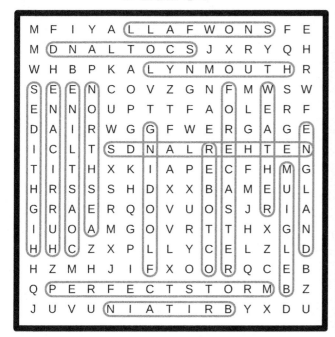

```
M F I Y A L L A F W O N S F E
M D N A L T O C S J X R Y Q H
W H B P K A L Y N M O U T H R
S E E N C O V Z G N F M W S W
E N N O U P T T F A O L E R F
D I A I R W G G F W E R G A E
I C L T S D N A L R E H T E N
I I T H X K I A P E C F H M G
T R S H D X X B A M E U I L
H A E R Q O V U O S J R G A N
G U O A M G O V R T H X L D
I H C Z X P L L Y C E L Z L B
H Z M H J I F X O O R Q C E B
Q P E R F E C T S T O R M B Z
J U V U N I A T I R B Y X D U
```

PAGE 99

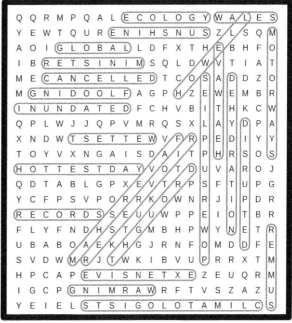

```
Q Q R M P Q A L E C O L O G Y W A L E S
Y E W T Q U R E N I H S N U S Z L S Q M
A O I G L O B A L L D F X T H E B H F O
I B R E T S I N I M S Q L D W V T I A T
M E C A N C E L L E D T C O S A D D S O
M G N I D O O L F A G P H Z E W E M B R
I N U N D A T E D F C H V B I T H K C W
Q P L W J J Q P V M R Q S X L A Y D P A
X N D W T S E T T E W V F R P E D I Y Y
T O Y V X N G A I S D A I T P H R S O J
H O T T E S T D A Y V O T D U V A R O J
Q D T A B L G P X E V T R P S F T U P G
Y C F P S V P O R R K O W N R J I P O T
R E C O R D S S E U U W P P E I O T T
F L Y F N D H S T G M B H P W Y N E F R
U B A B O A E K H G J R N E M O D N R K
S V D W M R J T W K I B V P W R X T M U
H P C A P E V I S N E T X E Z E U Q R M
I G C P G N I M R A W R F T V S Z A Z U
Y E I E L S T S I G O L O T A M I L C S
```

MORE GIFT IDEAS AVAILABLE FROM AMAZON

HOW TIMES HAVE CHANGED SINCE YOU WERE BORN

A HOW TIMES HAVE CHANGED book makes a great gift for anyone who is now celebrating a birthday, marriage or an anniversary. Packed full of the news and stories that filled the papers PLUS how we lived our lives from the 1950s right up to 2020.

Discover not just what happened but also the great sporting moments, fashion trends, what topped the music charts, cultural events, trivia and so much more.

Find out what was happening as you grew up, were at school, started work and raised a family.
- The major news stories of the times
- Changing fashion, music, and leisure
- How our homes were furnished and how we travelled
- See how the digital age transformed entertainment and our homes

Each book is packed with photographs to help you relive times gone by and bring memories flooding back.

Currently available from Amazon.
How Times Have Changed For Each Of These Years
1952, 1953, 1957, 1962, 1963, 1967, 1972, 1973.

More years are on their way so have a quick check by searching Amazon "Born in <YEAR>. How Times Have Changed.

The hardback book makes the most impressive and long lasting gift

Printed in Great Britain
by Amazon

33112448R00064